MUSEUMS

MASTERPIECES OF THE ARCHITECTURE IN THE WORLD

WHITE STAR PUBLISHERS

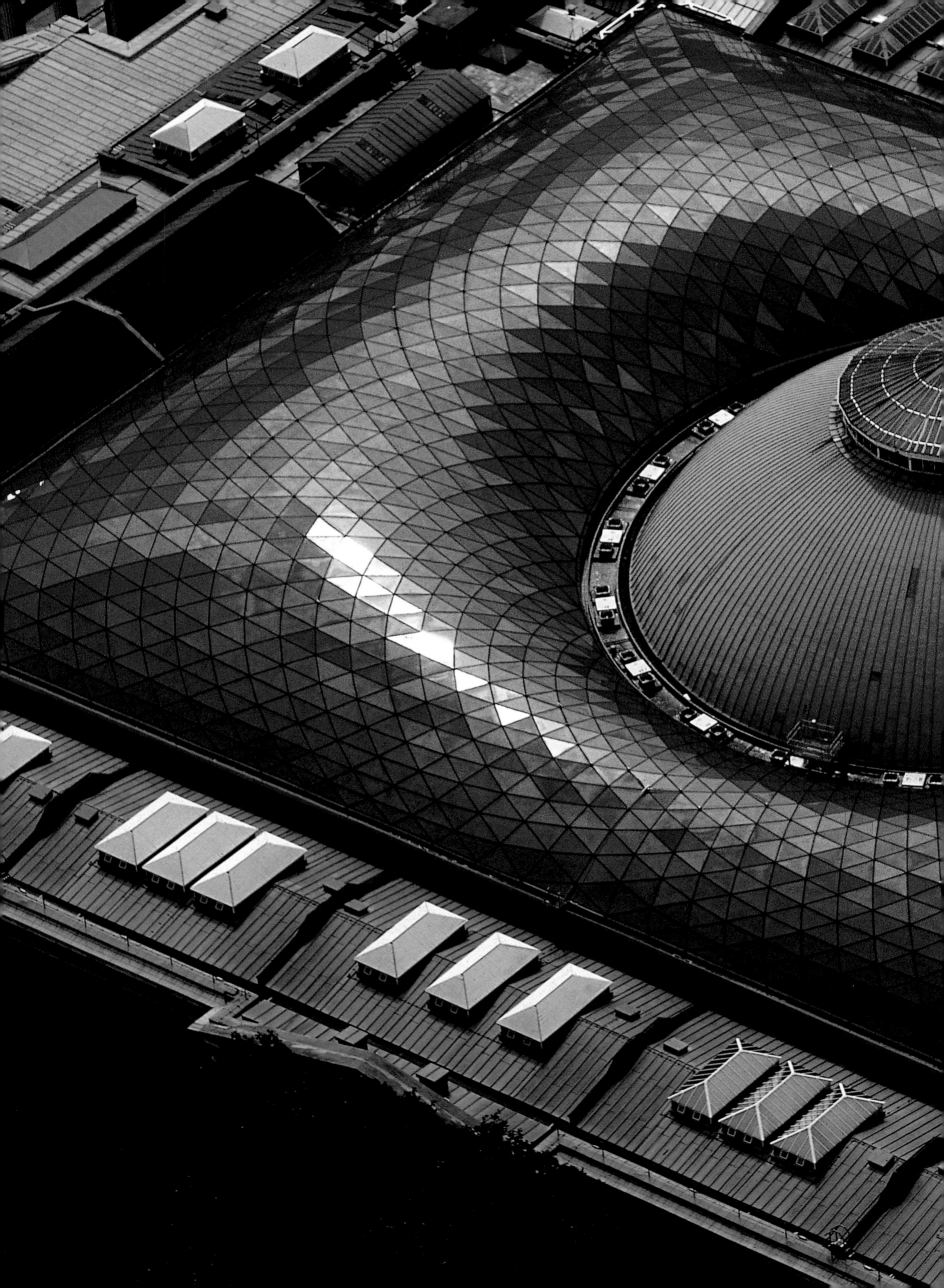

CONTENTS

TEXT
Giulia Camin

PROJECT EDITOR
Valeria Manferto De Fabianis

COLLABORATING EDITOR
Laura Accomazzo

GRAPHIC DESIGN
Paola Piacco

GRAPHIC LAYOUT
Stefania Costanzo

1 Sketch for the San Francisco Museum of Modern Art by Mario Botta, 1995.

2-3 The Louvre Pyramid by I.M. Pei, 1988.

4-5 The glass roof of the British Museum's Great Court by Norman Foster, 2000.

© 2007 White Star s.p.a.
Via Candido Sassone, 22/24 - 13100 Vercelli, Italy
www.whitestar.it

TRANSLATION: SARAH POINTING

ISBN 978-88-544-0280-5

Reprints:
1 2 3 4 5 6   11 10 09 08 07

Printed in China

INTRODUCTION

The history of world's museums is am incredibly fascinating topic. After having long been considered dusty repositories of memories of the past, today museums constitute the most effective and undisputed metaphor of society, past and present, whose changes and multiple facets they document. Museums are in fact extremely vital and dynamic places, capable of reinventing themselves continuously and keeping abreast of the times.

Just when the possible end of an institution too old to remain contemporary seemed to be drawing nigh, museums responded to the dreaded crisis by growing stronger and experiencing a blossoming and proliferation of unparalleled dimensions. An incredible number of cities throughout the world have established new museums since the final decades of the 20th century, driven by the most diverse motives. They have been aided by museum architecture, which has evolved and created new ways to shape these places of memory and collective identity, thus increasing their importance.

This book presents a comprehensive selection of museums from all over the world, recounting the history of their collections and the buildings that house them in stunning photographs showing their distinctive features. It thus accompanies the reader on a sort of journey back in time to discover the main figures in the development of museums over the ages. These fascinating stories not only allow us to trace the lives and talents of emperors, popes, private collectors, scholars and ordinary people who pursued the dream of founding them, but also to discover the remnants of the history of mankind, seen through the eyes of the men who wished to protect them from the ravages of time, study them and make them accessible to future generations.

Museology is an intricate blend of collecting, scientific and technical progress, architectural transformations and innovations, the study and history of civilizations of the past, and the arduous – and almost paradoxical – task of historicizing con-temporary time in the present. In the extensive overview offered here, museums appear in all their distinctive variety and heterogeneity, distinguished by strong individual personalities that underscore their different histories and paths. The guiding thread, uniting extremely different places and collections such as those examined in this book, is the wish to collect, conserve, display and hand down a legacy of the past, and this must be translated into the pleasure of knowledge, to be disclosed in the present and preserved for posterity. It is this aspect that unites the encyclopedic-style museums typical of the Enlightenment with their more modern, and often narrowly themed, counterparts.

Are museums mere containers? Certainly not: the story of those who founded, built and maintained them – and those who shaped their order and form by pursuing and organizing objects of economic and cultural value – allows us to explore the extraordinary and fertile ground of the history of the culture and memory of the various cultural identities that have arisen and exist around the world

When were museums born and how have they evolved over time? In order to trace the origins of this institution we must look to ancient history, when – as the term itself indicates – the museum was the Mouseion, the shrine of the Muses. Its role was that of a sacred temple, accessible only to priests. The first celebrated example in the history of this classical tradition is the famous building that was constructed by Ptolemy II Philadelphus in Alexandria in the 3rd century BC. It was a sort of ancient state cultural institution that housed valuable texts, manuscripts and rare books, but also sculptures and artistic and religious artifacts, and had the political role of bonding the new kingdom to the empire of Alexander the Great.

One of the earliest occasions on which the term "museum" was used to indicate a private collection of works of art was in the 16th century to refer to the extraordinary collection of portraits of famous men assembled by Paolo Giovio in his

---

6-7 *The Ambassadors' Staircase of the Hermitage Museum, St. Petersburg.*

8-9 *The Blanche and A.L. Levine Court of the Metropolitan Museum of Art, New York, 1939-1985.*

10 *The sign and logo of the Museum of Modern Art, New York.*

11 *Staircase at the entrance of the Kunsthistorisches Museum, Vienna, 1891.*

12 *The Museo de las Ciencias Príncipe Felipe, Valencia, by Santiago Calatrava, 2000.*

palace on Lake Como. In fact, Cosimo I paid tribute to him by naming his Galleria Gioviana in the Uffizi after him.

During the late Renaissance "cabinets of curiosities" became fashionable. The term was used to refer to peculiar private collections of unusual objects whose intention was not to catalog or classify items of scientific interest in order to place them in a logical context, but instead to display an array of amazing exhibits and miscellaneous curiosities with the sole aim of arousing wonder and marvel in the beholder. It was during the Enlightenment that the institution that embodies the modern idea of the museum was born. During this period numerous collections originally dedicated to specific themes were carefully expanded in the attempt to achieve the encyclopedic universality that characterized the age.

The thirst for systematically ordered and cataloged knowledge expressed by the museums of the Enlightenment perfectly reflected the quest of the first encyclopedias published during those years, including Denis Diderot's *Encylopédie* (1751). The Enlightenment museum became the quintessential temple of knowledge, in which all the most perfect products of art and nature must be displayed. It was at this precise moment in history that the museum assumed its most important social responsibility, which ensures that it still plays an important role for the community today. Indeed, it performs a vital educational and teaching function, conveying knowledge to and extending the horizons of all those who visit it.

Two unrivalled establishments in museum history were the product of this spirit: the British Museum in London, founded in 1759, and the Louvre Museum in Paris, which opened to the public in 1793. These two institutions are still universally acknowledged symbols of that thirst for universal knowledge and the repositories of vast precious collections that the museum for the first time opened to a wider public, irrevocably determining its function of social utility in a democratic form diametrically opposed to its elitist beginnings, when it was aimed at a select few.

The Enlightenment desire to represent all aspects of knowledge gave way to more specific collections and museums that concentrated their attention and efforts on the diversification of the various genres. This new orientation reflected historical, economic and social changes, expressing different political stances, and often becoming an instrument of power, no longer merely social, but also political, as testified by the museums founded under all forms of colonialist rule.

The fascinating vicissitudes of collectors and patrons that gave humanity places of incommensurable value are indissolubly bound up with the multifarious transformations of museum architecture, which experienced a period of great growth and fertility between the 20th and 21st centuries.

The modern era has witnessed a transformation of the temples of antiquity, the pantheons and corridors of noble palaces, the splendid royal residences in which the collections were originally status symbols, the cabinets of curiosities, and the veritable theaters of memory. Indeed, museums open to a wider audience require larger spaces for adequate enjoyment of their works, becoming public places and as such part of the modern industry of culture and entertainment.

The post-modern museums of our age have become cultural magnets, drawing huge crowds, becoming even more dynamic places in which the visitor not only finds collections to admire, but also events and situations in which to participate and interact.

Museums have thus become machines of cultural production, starting with the Centre Pompidou in Paris, with its futuristic and engineering-style structure of visible systems, designed by Renzo Piano and Richard Rogers and opened to the public in 1977.

However, the 21st century is also the age of spectacular architecture, which is exemplified by another fundamental building that has left its mark on the relationship between museum design and architecture. In 1997 a port city in the Basque Country of Spain, far off the beaten tourist track, became an international phenomenon imbued with new fame and prestige following the construction of the new museum of the Guggenheim Foundation. We are, of course, referring to Bilbao and the image with which the city itself is now universally identified: the incredible sculptural architecture of Frank O. Gehry, which not only houses, but actually competes with contemporary art.

Galleries or secular temples, once often aseptic and deliberately neutral in terms of display space, are now the focus of a fierce ongoing debate. On the one hand we find the spec-

15 *The National Gallery, London, by William Wilkins, 1838.*

16 *The Gugghenheim Museum of Art, Bilbao, by Frank O. Gehry, 1997.*

18-19 *The Kunsthistorisches Museum, Vienna, 1891.*

tacular architecture with alluring and seductive forms that is itself capable of attracting the public. Examples include Frank O. Gehry's Guggenheim Museum in Bilbao, but also Daniel Libeskind's Jewish Museum in Berlin, Moshe Safdie's Yad Vashem Museum in Jerusalem, Zaha Hadid's Vitra Design Museum in Weil am Rhein, Santiago Calatrava's Museu de les Ciències in Valencia, Jean Nouvel's Musée du Quai Branly in Paris, and UN Studio's Mercedes-Benz Museum in Stuttgart, all of which be admired in the magnificent photographs contained in this book.

The interesting aspect of these buildings derives from both the new methods of architectural design employed for their creation and the highly symbolic content of their forms, as exemplified by the work of Daniel Libeskind in Berlin and Moshe Safdie in Jerusalem. Both these museums are dedicated to the dramatic historical event of the Holocaust and are representative examples of buildings that have been designed not merely as places in which to display and preserve historical memories, but rather as true monuments and memorials.

There is also an array of equally monumental and spectacular museums with completely different aims. The architects of UN Studio designed the corporate Mercedes-Benz Museum in Stuttgart by reworking the manufacturer's three-pointed star, creating evocative spaces based on a double spiral, while Santiago Calatrava created an effectively monumental structure for his Museu de les Ciències in Valencia, and Jean Nouvel designed a striking new building to house the anthropological and ethnographic collections of the Musée du Quai Branly in Paris.

On the other hand, we find architecture pervaded by a simpler and linear display philosophy, devised for more neutral exhibition spaces. Examples include the work of many world-famous architects, including Mario Botta, and to a lesser extent Renzo Piano, Tadao Ando, Herzog and De Meuron, and Yoshio Taniguchi. The museums of these architects are contemporary cathedrals, which establish a spiritual bond with the space that they occupy, sometimes bordering on the immaterial.

In these cases we can use the popular description of "White Cube," denoting a building designed as a neutral and aseptic container whose sole aim is to enhance its contents. Another example is the celebration of the wide empty space of the Turbine Hall in the Tate Modern in London, where the Swiss architects Herzog and De Meuron implemented an industrial archaeology project aimed at making as few changes as possible in order to enhance the existing building. The fundamental use of natural light, which interpenetrates the spaces, characterizes both Yoshio Taniguchi's new Museum of Modern Art in New York and the work of Mario Botta, such as MART of Trento and Rovereto or the San Francisco Museum of Modern Art.

However, the history of all but the very latest museums is extremely stratified and the need to stay abreast of the times calls for a dynamic and vital approach that is reflected both in their cultural activities and programs and in their way of extending and rearranging their spaces. Consequently, during the 20th century, historic museums of the past started to commission extensions designed by famous contemporary architects, giving rise to a blend of modern and traditional. Examples include I.M. Pei's famous pyramid, which is now as much a symbol of the Louvre as the *Mona Lisa*; the Sainsbury Wing, designed by Robert Venturi and Denise Scott Brown for the National Gallery in London; Norman Foster's Great Court for London's British Museum; and Jean Nouvel's extension for the Reina Sofía in Madrid.

The selection presented in this book constitutes an overview, from east to west, of the world's leading museums, representing the most diverse collections and museum designs. They include the first encyclopedic-style institutions; museums pervaded by the allure of archaeology and anthropology that recount the great civilizations of the past; cult venues of art, from Renaissance to contemporary; and museums of natural history, science and technology, which house inestimable testimonies of the birth, evolution and progress not only of mankind, but also of the plant and vegetable kingdoms.

The museums of the world are thus ever-topical metaphors of humankind's thirst for knowledge and awareness that, over time, generated places where culture and knowledge could become a precious and democratic tool of individual and social enrichment.

20-21 Detail of the Natural History Museum, London, by Francis Fowke and Alfred Waterhouse, 1885.

22-23 The Musée du Quai Branly, Paris, by Jean Nouvel, 2005.

24-25 The Jewish Museum, Berlin, by Daniel Libeskind, 2001.

Kiasma Museum

HELSINKI, FINLAND

The Museum of Contemporary Art Kiasma in Helsinki opened to the public in May 1998. Its permanent collection of over 9000 works of visual art of all genres and themes is always accompanied by a vast array of projects, seminars, conferences and theatrical productions, making it both a gallery and an active cultural center engaged in promoting and introducing the general public to art and contemporary culture.

The striking building that houses it, and from which it draws its name, was designed by American Steven Holl, one of the greatest contemporary architects. The museum combines great attention to detail with constant spatial unity and fluidity. Despite being anti-spectacular and intertwined with the urban fabric and the surrounding environment in a modern but extremely natural way, it surprises visitors with its unpredictability. The name Kiasma is derived from the fact that the architectural structure of the building is based on the sculptural contrast between the ambiguous relationship of its intersecting parts, formed by a rectilinear block, towered over and enveloped by a curved, wave-like structure. Its simplicity is immediately perceptible in its form, materials and colors: the large, sinuous zinc, titanium and copper curve shapes the roof and the entire building, recalling the splendid natural environment that surrounds it and nearby Töölo Bay.

The dazzling white walls follow fluid curved lines and forms, creating 25 slightly oblique galleries, all of which are different. However, this diversity is always linked to the specific function of displaying the multifarious results of contemporary artistic experimentation. The unfolding sequence of these walls generates an infinite series of changing perspectives and viewpoints, imbuing the visitor with a continuous sense of discovery of the architecture and the works displayed within it. The relationship between natural light and the illumination of the interiors plays an essential role: each gallery is lit in a different way, ranging from artificial fluorescent lighting and intentionally half-lit areas to extremely bright ones with glazed openings that capture the horizontal natural light of northern latitudes.

26-27 The Museum of Contemporary Art Kiasma has been part of the Helsinki landscape since 1993 and is seamlessly integrated with its setting and the urban geometry. The sensitive curve of the building seems to embrace the city and its culture, hinting at implicit cultural links with the surrounding buildings (particularly the Finnish Parliament).

26 bottom and 27 top Kiasma is composed of two intersecting parts: a rectilinear block running parallel to the road (left in the photograph) and a curved one with a variable cross section, with one narrow end (right in the photograph) and another much wider, tunnel-like one, visible in the background on the left. This asymmetric structure is also partially reflected inside the building.

Kiasma Museum

28 Visitors to Kiasma experience constantly changing perspectives, which lend a dynamic quality to both the individual displays and the very concept of a museum. Its innovative architect, Steven Holl, expresses the rejection of set values, proposing alternative solutions.

29 The surprising perspectives inside Kiasma are the result of the architect's meticulous attention to the study of structural deformation in order to create non-static experiences. The aim is to immerse visitors in the architecture and contents of the building, amplifying their physical perception of them.

Kiasma Museum

30-31 and 31 Due to the asymmetry of the structure and its cross section, the distinctive tunnel-like curve of the southern body of the complex is echoed in the various rooms. All these features make the galleries perfectly adaptable to the various forms of contemporary art, while freeing the visitor from the constraints of a "regimented" museum visit. Holl's building has won the acclaim of public and critics alike, even in its name (which is so meaningful that it was already used to identify the project at the competition stage). It denotes a generic "crossing," in this case between the two parts of the building and between the city and the building itself, evoking their deep interactions and thus inserting the museum in the urban fabric and, emotionally, in the city's spirit.

British Museum

LONDON, UNITED KINGDOM

The British Museum, founded in 1759, is considered the oldest museum in the world. It was a product of the Enlightenment, to which it owes its encyclopedic nature and its aim to offer visitors an educational and instructive experience. Its history commenced in 1753, with the bequest of Sir Hans Sloane, a respected physician and naturalist who had succeeded Newton as the director of the Royal Society, and who was also a keen art collector.

Sloane was physician to George II and bequeathed to the king his collection of around 80,000 items, comprising a herbarium, a library, antiquities, precious stones and mathematical instruments in return for the payment of £20,000

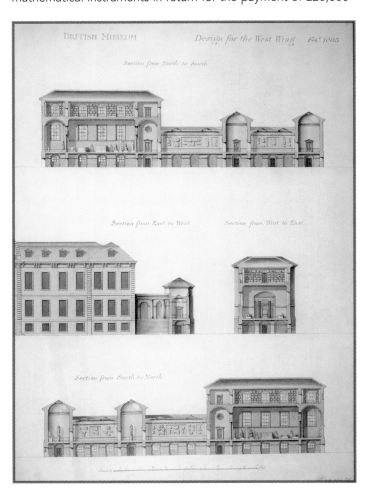

to his heirs. Parliament passed a special act – the British Museum Act – to raise these funds by means of a public lottery, and on January 15, 1759 the museum officially opened to the public in Montagu House, one of the finest late 17th-century buildings in London, which had been restored by the French architect Pierre Pouget. The act established that all the museum's collections, present or future, must be conserved and exhibited to the public, and that admission must be free and open to all. The British Museum was thus the first museum in the modern sense of the word, even though its original layout was more similar to the concept of the cabinet of curiosities, in which unordered collections of objects and works were housed. The growth of the collections required the expansion of the display areas, and in 1802 the Trustees decided to extend the museum with the construction of the Townley Gallery, which was completed in 1808. This Palladian-style building, designed by George Saunders, was used to display Charles Townley's classical sculpture collection and also to exhibit Egyptian antiquities.

The museum's collection of antiquities continued to grow, owing both to the constant excavations that it promoted all over the world and to a series of important acquisitions, such as the Parthenon Sculptures (1816) and the entire King's Library of George III, acquired in 1823. Further extension work was thus required, and construction commenced on the current premises, designed by Sir Robert Smirke and completed by his brother Sydney. The new building was a large rectangular structure surrounding an open courtyard and characterized by a great Neo-Classical-style façade, which symbolized the etymological origin and concept of the word "museum" as the temple of the Muses. The sculptures of the tympanum were the work of the famous sculptor Sir Richard Westmacott, who had studied under the great Canova.

32 top and 32-33 These aerial views reveal the front and back of the imposing structure of the British Museum. The tympanum and colonnades of the Neoclassical façade are visible on the right. The building forms a large quadrilateral around a huge inner courtyard.

32 bottom These cross sections show part of the project designed by architect George Saunders in 1803 for the extension of the museum. In 1808 the new wing (known as the Townley Gallery after the collector Charles Townley) was built to display classical and Egyptian antiquities.

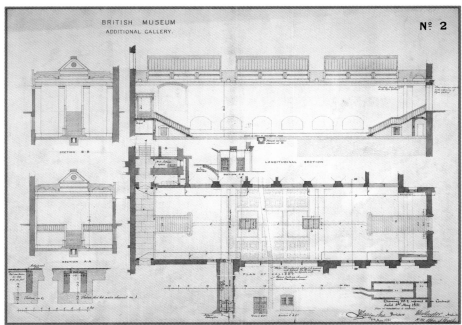

33 bottom The construction of the British Museum's Mausoleum Room, shown here in an 1882 plan and elevation, was completed the same year. It was built in an open space and designed by architect John Taylor to house the remains of the Mausoleum of Halicarnassus, acquired in 1856.

British Museum

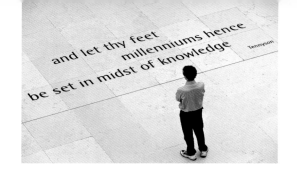

34-35, 35 top and center
The remarkable Great Court, opened to the public in 2000, was designed by architect Norman Foster, who won the competition held in 1994. The area covered by the glass dome is open to the public even after the galleries have closed.

35 bottom Stanley Smirke's original Reading Room, built between 1854 and 1857, has been restored and preserved beneath the innovative glass and steel dome. The circular building, clad in gray stone, is accessed by two large staircases. The area that is now occupied by Foster's magnificent creation is coherent with the museum's initial design by Robert Smirke, which also featured a large central courtyard. However, this was originally used to house offices and storerooms.

British Museum

36 top At the top of the majestic staircase visitors are greeted by the Discobolos, a Roman marble copy of the original statue by Myron.

36 center The museum's collection of ancient Egyptian art (the photograph shows the Egyptian sculpture room) is among its most famous and important treasures and includes the Rosetta Stone and the monumental bust of Ramesses II.

36 bottom The British Museum's Department of the Ancient Near East comprises exhibits from western Asia, which span an extremely wide chronological period.

36-37 The breathtaking dome of the Reading Room, designed by Sydney Smirke, was built in 1857 to create a suitable space to house the precious books formerly kept in the King's Library, completed in 1827.

This preliminary stage of construction ended in 1852, but was completed in 1857 with the addition of the Reading Room, a circular domed structure built in the center of the main courtyard. During the 19th century the museum was extended further with the White Wing (1882-1885), designed by Sir John Taylor. By this time the museum had become very popular with the public, and on public holidays great crowds flocked to view the exhibitions. This success was also due to the commitment of the museum's directors and curators, who researched, wrote and published guidebooks for visitors – the first of which was issued in 1808 – and popularized the collections with seminars and lectures.

During the 1880s the natural history collections were removed to what was then the South Kensington Museum, but which is now known as the Natural History Museum, thus leaving more room for the display of antiquities. Further construction work was undertaken between 1907 and 1914, and in 1931 Lord Duveen generously agreed to fund the building of a gallery designed by the American architect John Russell Pope to house the Parthenon Sculptures. The gallery was completed in 1939, but was not opened until 1962 because of war damage. The British Museum Press was subsequently founded and a public educational service established. The New Wing, designed by Colin St John Wilson, was opened in 1980, although it was only partially built due to a sudden cut in funding.

British Museum

38 top left The Sainsbury African Galleries display the bronze plaques from the palace of the Oba, the king of Benin city (in south Nigeria), collected during the British Punitive Expedition in 1897, along with many other precious artifacts such as ritual masks and heads.

38 top right The Department of Greek and Roman Antiquities was founded in 1886 and boasts a collection spanning a period stretching from the beginning of the Greek Bronze Age to the establishment of Christianity. It includes the room dedicated to portrait sculpture, featuring the busts of many emperors.

38 bottom The priceless collection of classical sculpture from the Acropolis in Athens was brought to Britain by Lord Elgin and consists largely of the decorations of the Parthenon. Indeed, about half of the Parthenon's friezes are currently housed in the British Museum.

39 Two monumental winged human-headed bulls were excavated in 1847 by the archaeologist Austen Henry Layard in Nimrud, in Iraq. One is now part of the British Museum's Assyrian collection, while its partner is housed in the Metropolitan Museum in New York.

Today an evocative new chapter has been added to the long history of the British Museum in the form of what has become one of its modern symbols: the spectacular Queen Elizabeth II Great Court. Built by the famous British architect Norman Foster, who won the competition to restore and rearrange the area of the historic Reading Room in 1994, the Great Court was inaugurated in 2000. A glass dome, composed of over 3000 uniquely shaped triangular panels, now covers the former open courtyard that is home to the perfectly restored Reading Room.

The museum's collections are organized according to historical, chronological and geographical criteria and housed in around 100 galleries that display exhibits and irreplaceable artifacts from all over the world. The treasures range from ethnographic collections dedicated to Africa and America, sections documenting the ancient Near East, the Chinese collection of the Asian section, and prehistoric finds from Britain and Europe. The museum also has extremely rich assembly of Egyptian antiquities – including a famous group of mummies and sarcophagi – and Greek and Roman art, as well as a section dedicated to Japanese decorative arts and paintings, a numismatic trove comprising 750,000 coins, and numerous works in the Prints and Drawings Gallery. One of the British Museum's most famous archaeological exhibits is the Egyptian black basalt tablet from the Ptolemaic period known as the Rosetta Stone, whose inscriptions in Greek, demotic and hieroglyphic provided the young French scholar Jean-François Champollion with the key to deciphering Egyptian hieroglyphs in 1822.

Victoria and Albert Museum
LONDON, UNITED KINGDOM

The Victoria and Albert Museum, the world's largest and most important museum of decorative arts, is home to an immense variety of collections, ranging from Renaissance bronzes to period costumes, huge tapestries, silks, porcelain, silverware, antique furniture and all kinds of jewelry. It was the first museum of its kind, predating other major museums of decorative arts in Vienna, Budapest, Nuremberg, Zagreb, Paris and elsewhere.

Two main figures were the driving forces behind the

40 top The latest metalworking technologies (the photograph is very early and dates from 1862) were employed for the construction of the South Kensington Museum, which later became the Victoria and Albert Museum.

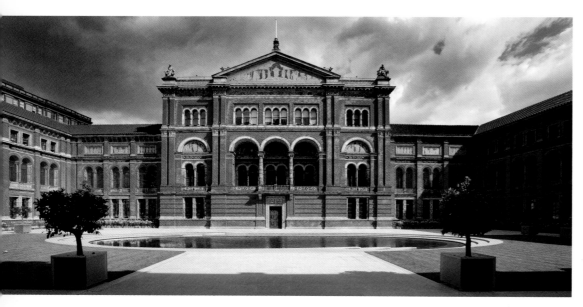

foundation and development of the museum: Henry Cole, who was also its first director and commissioned works of decorative art from several artists, and Richard Redgrave, an artist who became Art Superintendent in the Department of Practical Art. One of the most important events organized by Cole was the Great Exhibition of 1851, held at Crystal Palace. The exhibition was so successful that the proceeds allowed the purchase of a site for the new museum. Construction was completed in 1855 and the new premises opened to the public on June 22, 1857, as the South Kensington Museum. In addition to the collections housed in its former premises, Marlborough House, the new building also displayed recent patented inventions and a natural history collection. The most famous and precious exhibits included reproductions of Raphael's pilasters and lunettes from the Vatican Loggia and a mirror from the Bernal Collection.

40 bottom The John Madejski Garden, reopened in July 2005, has been transformed by Kim Wilkie. Its main feature is a stone-paved oval, which can be filled with water or left empty as required.

40-41 The Victoria and Albert Museum opened in South Kensington in 1857, but was given its current name in 1899 by Queen Victoria herself, who laid the building's first stone.

42 *Following three years of renovation work, the new Jameel Gallery, dedicated to Islamic and Middle Eastern Art, now houses a collection of over 400 objects dating from the 8th century to immediately before World War II, from an area ranging from Spain to Afghanistan.*

43 *top and bottom left The main entrance of the Victoria and Albert Museum is on Cromwell Road. A huge chandelier by the American artist Dale Chihuly hangs from the center of the dome in the entrance hall.*

43 *bottom right In the section dedicated to Asia, jewelry, textiles, artifacts, weapons, and paintings of the Mughal and British periods (16th to 19th centuries) are displayed in an evocative architectural setting.*

Victoria and Albert Museum

In 1862 two new buildings were constructed to house the rapidly expanding collection. The South Court combined decorated ironwork with murals, notably the cycle known as the "Kensington Valhalla," while the North Court was dedicated mainly to ceramics and casts. In 1865 all the exhibits were ordered on the basis of material. However, discussion regarding the most suitable layout – whether by chronology or type of object – became a recurring aspect of the history of the museum, which has reconsidered and debated its method of organization on numerous occasions.

A succession of events during the second half of the 19th century had a decisive influence on the development of the V&A: in 1869 Francis Fowke completed the construction work commenced in 1860, and the same period was marked by

important acquisitions, including casts of the Pórtico de la Gloria from Santiago de Compostela, which was displayed in parts due to lack of space, and Trajan's Column. In 1873 the Architectural Courts, designed by General Henry Scott, were opened, and at the end of the century (1899) the museum was renamed the Victoria and Albert Museum.

In 1909 the Aston Webb building was opened to the public and became the main entrance of the museum. The collection of casts, reproductions and original objects of European art was displayed in the West Court, while Indian architecture was displayed in the East Court. The museum's activities were accompanied by continuous study and research, and employees of the V&A wrote many contemporary publications on the decorative arts.

44 top The museum's collection of casts is one of its highlights. Highlights include a copy of Michelangelo's David, presented to Queen Victoria in 1857 by the Grand Duke of Tuscany. The Queen immediately donated the statue to the South Kensington Museum, now known as the Victoria and Albert.

44 bottom The Green Dining Room, or the Morris Room, was decorated by William Morris' firm Morris, Marshall, Faulkner & Co. in 1861. Inspired by the decorative reinterpretation of medieval art, it features typical stylistic motifs of the period, such as the pre-Raphaelite figures on a gold ground by the artist Edward Burne-Jones.

44-45 The Victoria and Albert Museum is also home to Antonio Canova's famous sculptural group depicting the classic theme of the Three Graces (1814–17). The work was commissioned by John Russell, the 6th Duke of Bedford, who was captivated by the beauty of the Three Graces that Canova had carved for the Empress Josephine, the estranged wife of Napoleon.

Victoria and Albert Museum

The same year also witnessed the opening of the Octagon Court, where exhibitions mixing objects from different departments were staged for the first time.

The V&A buildings suffered extensive damage during World War II, but following an initial period of closure, the museum reopened in 1940, with the intention of encouraging public morale at such a difficult time. Ever since then the galleries have been divided into two types: those ordered according to the style, period or origin of the exhibits, and those that retained a materials-based approach. Major exhibitions, regularly mounted since the 1970s, are still a feature of this very active museum and cultural center.

46-47 The 90-ft (27-m) Waterloo Gallery at Apsley House, the home of the first Duke of Wellington, was formerly managed by the V&A as part of the Wellington Museum.

47 top The classical-style Ceramic Staircase was richly decorated with mosaics, painting and ceramics between 1865 and 1871. Its subjects include mythological themes and allegories of the Arts and Sciences, which were considered appropriate for an institution dedicated to education.

47 center The Norfolk House Music Room features the original, richly adorned panels and ceiling from the music room of Norfolk House, the Duke of Norfolk's London home, which was demolished in 1938.

47 bottom The National Art Library at the Victoria and Albert Museum is a major public reference library for readers interested in the fine and decorative arts. The architecture of its reading room is simple and austere.

48-49 and 49 The National Gallery, London's most important art gallery, was founded in 1824 by a group of citizens, collectors and art dealers.

The Neoclassical-style building designed by William Wilkins is located in the city center, in Trafalgar Square, where it opened to the public in 1838.

National Gallery
LONDON, UNITED KINGDOM

The National Gallery is one of the most recent national art galleries in the world. It was founded in 1824 and, unlike other equally important national museums, was not derived from a royal collection, but was established from the outset as a public museum with free admission for all citizens. The most interesting aspect of its history regards the formation of its collection. Indeed, the gallery was not founded to house collections composed according to a specific plan, but due to the interest of a group of upper-class merchants and collectors who dealt shrewdly on the art market with the aim of creating a body of extraordinary masterpieces.

The gallery was founded during the reign of George IV, a cultured sovereign and collector who undoubtedly contributed to the general interest in the project. Parliament, urged by the Prime Minister, Lord Liverpool, decided to allocate a large fund for the purchase, conservation and display of collections of paintings of public importance. The first acquisition that Lord Liverpool promoted consisted of 38 works belonging to the collection of the recently deceased banker John Julius Angerstein. Subsequently other patrons rushed to donate their collections to the gallery, thus forming the core of the new national collection, which was opened to the public on May 10, 1824 in Angerstein's house. The exhibition featured works by great masters such as Claude Lorrain, Rembrandt, Rubens, Van Dyck, Hogarth, Raphael and Sebastiano del Piombo.

National Gallery

50 top The National Gallery's East Wing was extended with a project commenced in 2003 by architects Dixon Jones, and culminated in the reopening of the Main Portico Entrance on Trafalgar Square in 2005 and the opening of the Sir Paul Getty Entrance.

50 bottom The National Gallery's new Sainsbury Wing was designed to house the collection of Renaissance painting and was the first building in Europe by the American architects Robert Venturi and Denise Scott Brown.

51 The Sainsbury Wing, clad with Portland Stone (a white-gray limestone), is connected to the main building of the National Gallery by a circular bridge and houses 16 rooms covering an area of over 30,000 sq. ft (2790 sq. m).

National Gallery

52 The staircase hall of the East Wing is topped with a dome and its walls and ceiling feature a polychromatic decorative scheme by J.D. Crace, a well-known interior designer of the late Victorian period.

53 top The attention to natural light (the photograph shows a skylight in Room 11) reveals the relatively recent design of the building, which was devised as a museum from the outset.

53 bottom left As part of the 2004 development, the Central Hall was refurbished and reinstated as a picture gallery and now houses some of the most important paintings of the National Gallery's collection.

53 bottom right A school party admires one of the National Gallery's most important paintings: The Family of Darius before Alexander by Paolo Veronese.

However, the relatively small and shabby building was fiercely criticized by the London press, which mercilessly and unfairly compared it to the grandiose complex of the renowned Louvre in Paris.

Among the benefactors who enabled the National Gallery to expand its collections were the painter and art patron Sir George Beaumont, and William Holwell Carr, who left the gallery his collection comprising works by Rembrandt and the famous Saint George and the Dragon by Tintoretto. These gifts were followed by further acquisitions conducted by a board of trustees formed in 1825, including masterpieces such as The Madonna of the Basket by Correggio and Bacchus and

Ariadne by Titian. In 1831 Parliament finally decided to construct a new building on a site in Trafalgar Square, chosen for its accessibility. The collections were expanded further during the Victorian period, bringing the gallery even greater prestige. In 1840 Queen Victoria married Prince Albert, who was a great lover of ancient and modern painting and dedicated considerable effort to emphasizing the importance of a national gallery. In 1842 the gallery acquired one of its most famous works: The Arnolfini Portrait by Jan van Eyck

The building was inspired by Carlton House, which formerly occupied the site, and Wilkins reused several of its columns in the porticoes on the eastern and western sides of the façade.

During the 1850s a series of controversies stemming from the need to restore several badly preserved works damaged by pollution led to an investigation of the conduction of the gallery and the suitability of its premises. However, it was felt that moving the National Gallery from its historical seat in central London, would undermine public access, and so the works remained in Trafalgar Square, although the number of visitors was restricted. Under the direction of Sir Charles Eastlake, who dedicated greater attention to the quality and renown of acquisitions, the National Gallery extended its collection with many more paintings, including masterpieces of Italian art, such as *An Allegory with Venus and Cupid* by Bronzino, *The Family of Darius before Alexander* by Veronese, *The Battle of San Romano* by Paolo Uccello and *The Baptism of Christ* by Piero della Francesca, as well as numerous works by William M. Turner.

In 1868, following a spate of fierce criticism directed at the building, architect E.M. Barry was asked to submit designs for a new one. However, his project was never built, and the existing building was instead extended with a new east wing and the famous dome. In 1903 the National Art Collections Fund was established with the aim of bringing to Britain as many as possible of the works on the international art market. During World War II the gallery was closed and its paintings hidden in safer locations. However, the building was damaged during air raids and deemed unfit to house the collections. In 1946 Philip Hendy was appointed director and subsequently supervised a project aimed at creating new exhibition areas and restoring the damaged ones. The building work continued for many years and the Northern Extension was completed only in 1975. The last great stage in the gallery's expansion dates back to the 1990s, with the construction of the Sainsbury Wing, named after the family who financed it. The Sainsbury Wing was designed by architect Robert Venturi and was inaugurated in 1991 by the Queen. It houses the section dedicated to Early Renaissance painting.

Today the National Gallery continues to maintain all its original intentions: it is open to the public with free admission and is home to works of inestimable historical and artistic importance, including *Saint Jerome in his Study* by Antonello da Messina, *Venus and Mars* by Sandro Botticelli, *The Virgin of the Rocks* by Leonardo da Vinci, *Portrait of a Lady Inspired by Lucretia* by Lorenzo Lotto, and many others besides. Visitors can also admire the 19th-century works acquired through the Hugh Lane Bequest and the fund established by Samuel Courtauld, including paintings by Jean-Auguste-Dominique Ingres, Pierre-Auguste Renoir, Georges Seurat, Edouard Manet and Paul Cézanne.

National Gallery

54 and 54-55 The dignified Georgian refinement of the National Gallery's décor and its architecture, along with the commendable rationality of its design, never fail to fascinate visitors, however intent they may be on admiring the works on display. The photographs show Room 9, with works by Paolo Veronese and the Venetian school, and Room 15, with a painting by Claude (top left page); a view from Room 58 to Room 57, showing works by Pollaiuolo and Botticelli (bottom); and, right, the Central Hall. One of the first visitors to admire these rooms was the daughter of Edward, Duke of Kent, the future Queen Victoria.

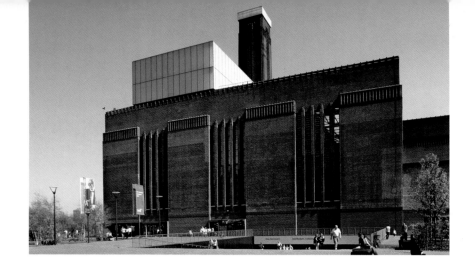

Tate Modern

LONDON, UNITED KINGDOM

56 top The Tate Modern is housed in London's former Bankside Power Station, designed by Gilbert Scott. The building was commenced in 1947, but was not completed until 1963. Its turbines produced much of the capital's electricity until its closure during the 1980s.

56 center and bottom The longitudinal section of the building and the plan of the ground floor show the project implemented by Swiss architectural firm Herzog and De Meuron between 1997 and 1999.

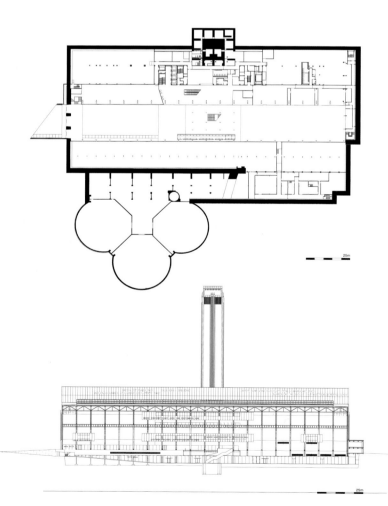

London's Tate Modern dominates the Thames from Bankside, and its presence is effectively marked by the "lightbeam," which is visible from a great distance. It is a very new museum. In 1994 an international architectural competition was held for the design of what was soon to become one of the world's most important and consecrated cathedrals of contemporary art. The prestigious Swiss firm of Herzog and De Meuron won the award, and its four partners (Jacques Herzog, Pierre de Meuron, Harry Gugger and Christine Binswanger) were commissioned to renovate and convert the giant Bankside Power Station into a gallery suitable for housing the very latest forms of art.

The power station was designed by Sir Gilbert Scott (who also designed Battersea Power Station) and built between 1947 and 1963. It was in use until the 1980s, when it was closed, like many other buildings in this less than prime urban area. During the 1990s London experienced a particularly fertile period of artistic and cultural development, and an urgent need to build a "home for contemporary art" was perceived. Scott's power station was chosen as the ideal premises for the new branch of the historic Tate Britain, formerly known as the Tate Gallery. The latter was opened in 1897 and became world famous for its extraordinary collections of art, spanning the period from 1500 to the present day. It was named after its founder, the sugar magnate Sir Henry Tate, who financed its construction at Millbank and gave it his collection of British art. Today the Tate is a dynamic family of four galleries: the other two are the Tate St Ives (in Cornwall, southwestern England) and the Tate Liverpool. The Tate Modern, opened to the public in 2000, is the youngest and most contemporary.

Herzog and De Meuron's winning design had the great merit of retaining much of the building's essential character, making only small but essential changes. Indeed, the project has preserved the building's distinctive red-brick shell, characteristic of British industrial architecture, which has been brought up to date with a sole external addition: the "lightbeam" roof structure that has become the symbol of its new look and a conceptual link with its former function.

57 The Tate Modern, which has become a cult venue for the exhibition of contemporary art in London, stands on the bank of the Thames by the Millennium

Bridge. Swiss landscape architects Keinast Vogt Partner designed a little wooded area, composed of around 600 trees arranged in orderly rows, outside the gallery.

58-59 One of the main characteristics distinguishing the work of the firm of Herzog and De Meuron is their dematerialization of the traditional concept of architecture, constructing and enhancing space without resorting to excessively invasive solutions.

58 bottom and 59 top The gallery's Café 2 is located on Level 2, along with the Starr Auditorium, the Seminar Room and a small shop. The Tate Modern Restaurant (Level 7) and the Members Room (Level 6) offer visitors and clients breathtaking views over the Thames, Saint Paul's Cathedral and the London skyline.

Tate Modern

59 bottom The huge, evocative red PVC sculptural installation entitled Marsyas, created by Indian artist Anish Kapoor (b. 1954) for the Tate Modern in 2002, was the third in The Unilever Series of commissions for the gallery's Turbine Hall.

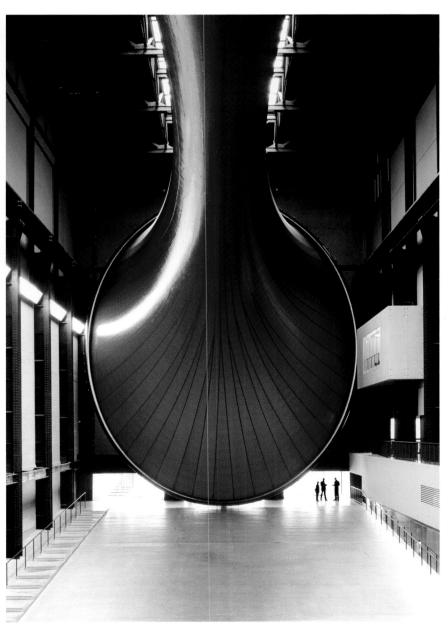

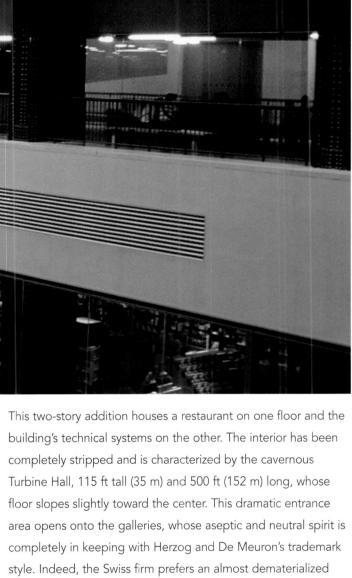

This two-story addition houses a restaurant on one floor and the building's technical systems on the other. The interior has been completely stripped and is characterized by the cavernous Turbine Hall, 115 ft tall (35 m) and 500 ft (152 m) long, whose floor slopes slightly toward the center. This dramatic entrance area opens onto the galleries, whose aseptic and neutral spirit is completely in keeping with Herzog and De Meuron's trademark style. Indeed, the Swiss firm prefers an almost dematerialized architecture to spectacular and obtrusive forms that compete with the works on display.

The first series of exhibitions the Tate Modern presented in the Turbine Hall underscored the success of an architectural project capable of creating a particularly suitable space for enhancing multiform – and often difficult to display –

Tate Modern

contemporary artistic creations, from the enormous bronze spider sculpture by Louise Bourgeois, exhibited for the opening in 2000, and the work of Juan Muñoz (2001) to Bruce Nauman's sound installations in the "Raw Materials" exhibition (2004), Anish Kapoor's spectacular and colossal *Marsyas* (2002), and also Olafur Eliasson's highly evocative *Weather Project* (2003). The galleries, on the other hand, are more conventional in terms of museum design, which nonetheless underscores their adherence to the intentionally neutral "white cube" tradition. They have hosted a series of great events, many of which have subsequently become traveling exhibitions, such as the highly praised "Matisse Picasso" show presented in 2002. The permanent collection features examples of various movements, from Fauvism to the Surrealist avant-garde, with works by Salvador Dalí, Joan Miró, Max Ernst and René Magritte, masterpieces by Matisse and Picasso, sculptures by Naum Gabo, works by Alberto Giacometti, Pop Art pieces by Andy Warhol and Roy Lichtenstein, examples of American Abstract Expressionism, with Jackson Pollock's action paintings, and Mark Rothko's *Seagram Murals*, as well as many key works by Minimalist and Conceptual artists.

60 top The galleries and exhibition areas are formed by mobile walls that can be moved to rearrange the areas according to layout requirements and the size and types of works to be displayed.

60 bottom Scottish artist Douglas Gordon (b. 1966) is one of the contemporary artists featured in the permanent collection. In this installation Gordon has altered a photograph of James Mason to create movement from a still.

60-61 One of the most interesting aspects of the layout of the permanent collection, which occupies an area of over 150,000 sq. ft (13,950 sq. m), is that it is arranged according to theme rather than the usual chronological sequence. The photographs show works by René Magritte, Giulio Paolini and Jean Arp, among others.

61 bottom Herzog and De Meuron deliberately maintained the apparently gloomy style of the typical British industrial architecture of the mid-20th century, which contrasts with the brightness of the building's huge interiors, where the works of art are completely free to express themselves, either individually or in synergy.

62-63 The exterior of the Natural History Museum is very imposing, suggesting the importance of the collection that it houses. Its parallel pitched roofs, clearly visible in the photograph, mark each of the building's six main galleries.

62 bottom A series of five terracotta panels exemplifies the general inspiration for the decorative details of the museum, which focus on the depiction of the most diverse creatures of the natural world, both living and fossil.

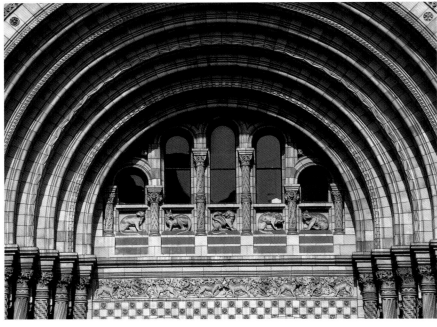

63 top A series of columns reveals the ingenious and attractive system used to hide the real structure of the building, constituted by a metal "skeleton."

63 bottom The building is richly decorated in an eclectic style, typical of the late Victorian period and makes extensive use of terracotta bricks, which offered excellent resistance to the damp and sooty climate of Victorian London.

Natural History Museum

LONDON, UNITED KINGDOM

The Natural History Museum in London is the premier institution of its kind in the world. Its collections comprise over 70 million biological and geological specimens and are displayed in its stunning South Kensington premises, not far from two other London museums: the Science Museum and the Victoria and Albert Museum.

The museum building opened to the public in 1881, but the origins of the original core of the collections date back to 1753, when the scientist Sir Hans Sloane left his large personal collection of natural exhibits to the nation. The bequest comprised around 80,000 animal and vegetable specimens, a priceless herbarium, and a huge library of rare works, which Sir Hans had pieced together during his lifetime. At the time it was the largest private collection in Europe and initially became one of the core components of the British Museum in London, which opened to

the public in 1759. Sloane's collection was subsequently joined by other equally precious exhibits, such as those collected by botanist Joseph Banks on his 1768 voyage to Australia with Captain Cook aboard the HMS *Endeavour*. The expansion of the British Museum's natural history section led to an increasingly urgent need for a separate museum dedicated solely to natural history and science exhibits. The idea was strongly supported by the Superintendent of the British Museum's natural history collection, Sir Richard Owen, who drew up a plan of proposals for new ways of ordering and displaying it. A site was chosen in South Kensington and the architect Francis Fowke was commissioned to design the museum. Following his death in 1865, the contract was awarded to the Manchester architect Alfred Waterhouse, who designed the current building.

The construction techniques employed by Waterhouse were

64 and 65 bottom The Natural History Museum is equally sumptuous inside and conveys an air of sanctity, in accordance with

the positivist thought of its time. The photographs show two views of the huge Central Hall, a "Cathedral of Nature."

65 top In contrast with the rational display systems used by almost all museums today, the Natural History Museum's collections retain a certain chaotic

quality that has its own charm. The number of exhibits is simply staggering: around 70 million, making it the richest museum of its kind in the world.

Natural History Museum

highly innovative for the period, and the building features an iron-and-steel frame concealed by a series of columns and arches richly decorated with plant and animal motifs, reflecting the contents and function of the museum itself.

The building was constructed in an eclectic style; the entrance is set in a portal in the center of the imposing façade, flanked by two soaring towers. All the mineral and natural history collections were moved to this building, which opened to the public in 1881 as the Natural History Museum. The collections also featured numerous exhibits from scientific expeditions, including the round-the-world voyage of the *Challenger* (1872-76), Captain Scott's Antarctic expedition (1910), the museum's own trip to the dinosaur-bearing deposits of Tanganyika (1924-31), and John Murray's Indian Ocean expedition (1933-34).

The Natural History Museum's collections were further enriched by the bequests of many collectors and amateur natural historians. The largest and most significant of these was the

collection amassed by the keen ornithologist Lionel Walter, Baron Rothschild, who founded the first zoological museum in Tring, Hertfordshire. In addition to countless specimens of butterflies, carefully stuffed mammals, birds and giant tortoises, Rothschild also possessed a large scientific library.

The museum is also home to the Alfred Wallace Collection, which belonged to the great British scientist born in 1823. It not only comprises specimens of natural history but also documents, papers and articles illustrating Wallace's scientific studies on the theory of evolution by natural selection. The evocative halls of the Natural History Museum allow visitors to admire five main collections: botany, entomology, mineralogy, paleontology and zoology. The museum's priceless scientific and cultural legacy includes insects, mammals, birds, prehistoric fossils, algae, ferns, mosses, lichens, seeds, rocks, minerals and meteorites, and indeed the most famous specimen of all – a majestic 85-foot-tall Diplodocus skeleton, which welcomes visitors in the entrance hall.

66 top Construction of the current premises of the Rijksmuseum was completed in 1883 by architect Petrus Josephus Hubertus Cuypers (1827–1921), who won the competition announced for the project and was appointed national architect of museum buildings.

Rijksmuseum

AMSTERDAM, NETHERLANDS

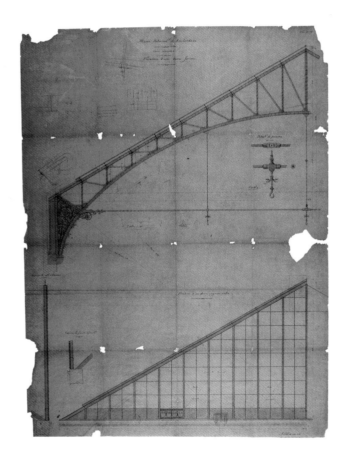

The Rijksmuseum in Amsterdam is the largest and most revered museum in the Netherlands and home to an extraordinary collection of great Dutch art of all periods. The museum was actually founded in The Hague, where it was housed in the Huis ten Bosch. It opened to the public for the first time in 1800 as the National Art Gallery and displayed the early collections of works belonging to William V of Orange (1748-1806), the Netherlands' last stadtholder (ruler), consisting mainly of Dutch paintings dating from the 1600s, the "Golden Century" of Dutch art.

The turning point for the museum came in 1805, when Holland became part of the Napoleonic Empire. The following year Napoleon appointed his brother Louis Bonaparte as King of Holland. Louis commenced a program of expanding and developing the capital; he recognized the need for projects capable of emphasizing the status of Amsterdam as the country's most important city. For the same reason, Louis firmly resolved to establish a museum, whose foundation was formally sanctioned on April 28, 1808. It was housed in the former town hall – a splendid 17th-century building renamed the Royal Palace – where the collections from The Hague were transferred to create the Royal Museum. One of the museum's most important masterpieces, Rembrandt's *Night Watch* (1642), was acquired at this time. Following a short crisis when Holland briefly became a French province, the museum started to expand with important acquisitions, also promoted by King William I of the Netherlands, who ascended the throne in 1813 and gave the museum a new name: Rijks Museum.

66 bottom These photographs show two prints housed in the Netherlands Architecture Institute in Rotterdam. Left, a detail of one of the animal and vegetable motifs created for one of the finest features of the

decorative scheme of the Rijksmuseum: the painted decorations that adorn the walls, both inside and outside. Right, a detail of the metal frame used for a structural part of the museum's courtyard.

66-67 The architectural style of Cuypers' building fully reflects the spirit and the typical historical and artistic characteristics of the mid- and late-18th-century Netherlands, while also featuring Gothic and Renaissance stylistic details.

After a series of ups and downs, during which the museum changed its name several times, the premises were transferred to the Trippenhuis, a 17th-century mansion, and unified with the existing Print Room. However, it was not until 1885 that the museum was transferred to its current home. The architect Peter Joseph Hubert Cuypers was commissioned to design the new premises, and between 1875 and 1883 built a traditional palace in contemporary Dutch architectural style with the eclectic addition of Gothic and Renaissance elements. The building was altered and extended in various stages during the 20th century. The collections were also expanded and the most representative Dutch works were acquired at the end of the 19th century. Indeed, during this period the museum acquired a series of

paintings formerly used for anatomy lessons from the Surgeons' Guild, over 200 paintings by the Flemish school from the prominent Van der Hoop Museum in Amsterdam, and other important masterpieces from the Vereniging Rembrandt, an association founded in 1883 by wealthy art lovers to finance purchases.

The Rijksmuseum's current collection includes a magnificent section dedicated to Rembrandt and the Delft school, where visitors can admire 18 masterpieces by the great Dutch painter, including the aforesaid *Night Watch*, *Self-Portrait as a Young Man* (1628) and *Portrait of Maria Trip* (1639). The museum also boasts a section of 17th-century Dutch painting, dedicated to three most famous schools of painting of the Golden Century: those of Haarlem, Amsterdam and Utrecht.

DUTCH REPUBLIC · Never has the Netherlands been so wealthy and powerful as in the 17th century, the Golden Age. In the Eighty Years' War (1568-1648) the Dutch expelled their Spanish rulers and established an independent state. Unlike most of Europe, the new country was not a kingdom but a republic. Power was in the hands of the burghers. · It was not long before the Republic, one of the Seven United Provinces became one of Europe's leading nations, constantly warring with its neighbours. The country grew rich on trade and shipping. Dutch vessels sailed the world's oceans. In the Dutch Republic, produce and raw materials from across the world were stocked, processed and distributed. Merchants amassed fortunes and art and culture flourished.

Rijksmuseum

68-69 and 69 Sculptures, paintings, ceramics and numerous works of applied art mingle in the halls of the Rijksmuseum. However, the museum is renowned above all for its large, priceless and highly representative collection of 17th-century Dutch painting. The photographs show the large canvas by Frans Hals and Pieter Codde known as The Meagre Company (1637), and one of the rooms dedicated to Flemish art.

The rich collection of Dutch works, spanning a period from the 15th to the 19th century, also features masterpieces of art contiguous with Flemish production, but with a greater propensity for genre figures – from the still lifes of Pieter Claeszoon and Adriaen Coorte, to the landscapes of Van Goyen and Ruisdael – in addition to Flemish masterpieces by Rubens, Van Dyck and Jan Bruegel. Other sections are dedicated to foreign schools of painting, with works by Francisco Goya and Italian masters, including Sandro Botticelli, Jacopo Tintoretto, Paolo Veronese and Giovanni Battista Tiepolo. However, the museum also has equally extraordinary collections of sculpture, ceramics and decorative arts, with almost 45,000 pieces of Delft pottery, Meissen porcelain and examples of Chinese ceramics. Not to be omitted is the museum's renowned Print Room.

70-71 The Pergamon Museum is part of the Museuminsel complex that grouped together Berlin's most important history museums on the island on the Spree River from the 19th century, housing them in the buildings designed by Friedrich August Stüler.

70 bottom World War II caused extensive structural damage to Berlin's museums. The Pergamon Museum was severely hit and the subsequent rebuilding work did not allow it to reopen until 1954.

Pergamon Museum

BERLIN, GERMANY

The Pergamon Museum in Berlin is home to one of the most renowned collections of ancient art in the world. It belongs to the city's Staatliche Museen (State Museums) and is part of the Museuminsel (Museum Island), home to Berlin's most important museums. Prior to World War II, the precious collections now displayed in the Pergamon Museum were divided between three museums: the Old (Altes) Museum, the New (Neues) Museum and the Pergamon Museum, which was dedicated to Greek and Roman architecture and housed the magnificent Pergamon Altar. The three buildings were independent, but connected, allowing visitors to admire irreplaceable relics of ancient Greek, Roman, Etruscan and Cypriot art.

In 1830 the Old Museum was founded to house the original nucleus of these collections. It was designed by Karl Friedrich Schinkel and built in front of the Lustgarten, opposite Berlin Castle. The museum's collections consisted of acquisitions made by Frederick II (1740-86) and Frederick William II (1786-97) of Prussia. During the late 18th century they were housed in the Castle and subsequently transferred to the new building designed by Schinkel. The most important room of the Old Museum, designed to house antique sculpture, had a dome modeled on the Pantheon in Rome. The other rooms contained ancient Greek and Roman statuary and a distinguished collection of medieval sculpture. The Antiquarium housed examples of the decorative arts, such as vases, bronzes, pottery and works set with semiprecious stones. The educational intent of the museum was always enthusiastically pursued, particularly by the archaeologist Eduard Gerhard, who systematically documented and cataloged the exhibits and conducted a shrewd policy of acquisitions aimed at filling the geographical and chronological gaps in the collections. The new acquisitions included Etruscan works obtained directly from the excavations at Vulci and Tarquinia.

When the museum's display space became insufficient, the architect Friedrich August Stüler was commissioned to design a second building, known as the New Museum. It was built between 1843 and 1855 and housed the plaster casts and the many Egyptian antiquities. These collections continued to expand, fueled by the large-scale excavation campaigns the museum conducted in Greece and Turkey. Another new museum building was designed by Alfred Messel and completed by Ludwig Hoffman on the Kupfergraben side of Museum Island. It became home to the section dedicated to ancient Greek, Roman and Near Eastern architecture, and also featured faithful reconstructions designed for educational purposes. This building became the Pergamon Museum. It housed the most precious and famous work of all: the Pergamon Altar, the most important monumental Greek altar ever discovered, whose west side was rebuilt in the museum's central hall. The marble altar, dating from 164-156 BC, consists of an extraordinary frieze, over 6.5 ft (2 m) high, a flight of steps extending 65 ft (20 m), and a series of Ionic columns that supported an entablature depicting gods, griffons and horses, with over 100 figures engaged in dramatic struggles. The museum also houses the propylaea of the Sanctuary of Athena of Pergamon and the columns of the Temple of Athena of Priene. Another outstanding architectural exhibit is the market gate of Miletus, which dates back to Hadrian's time.

---

71 top Construction of the Pergamon Museum in Berlin (shown here in 1914) commenced around 1910. The work was directed by Alfred Messel and Ludwig Hoffmann, and was not completed until 1930.

71 bottom The Pergamon Museum is composed of three wings: the first two to be built were inspired by classical temples, while the style of the central block, built to house the Pergamon Altar, is more austere.

Pergamon Museum

72-73 The Ishtar Gate (4th century BC) from Babylon has been partially reconstructed in the section of the museum dedicated to the Near East.

73 top The Market Gate of Miletus, built during Roman times, is one of the many architectural reconstructions that make this museum unique.

73 bottom The awe-inspiring Great Altar of Zeus (164–156 BC) was found near Pergamon, in Asia Minor, during the excavation campaign conducted between

1878 and 1886 by the Berlin Museums, directed by archaeologist Karl Humann. Its transfer to Berlin required the construction of a suitably large new building.

During World War II the three museums suffered extensive damage and several of the collections of the New Museum were moved to a wing of the Pergamon Museum. However, they were not displayed properly until many years later, following renovation work carried out during the 1980s.

The Pergamon Museum is also home to the Museum of the Ancient Near East (Vorderasiatisches Museum), established in 1899 as a separate body. In 1926 its collections were incorporated into the Pergamon Museum, where their prestige and dimensions were greatly augmented by a series of donations, acquisitions and objects from digs, including the important excavation projects in Babylon and Assur. One of the most extraordinary attractions of this part of the museum is the partial reconstruction of the Processional Way of Babylon, a sort of corridor over 650 ft (200 m) long, as it appeared in the 6th century BC. This section houses many exceptional exhibits documenting a period of history spanning around 6000 years.

The chronological structure of the Pergamon Museum and the educational emphasis that has always been its hallmark not only allow visitors to admire the works on display, but also to deepen their knowledge of the Assyrian, Sumerian and Babylonian civilizations.

74 top *The alternating succession of solids and voids formed between the broken lines of the Jewish Museum in Berlin create a series of gaps that architect Daniel Libeskind has used to emphasize the importance of empty space as an evocative and effective symbol of absence.*

Jewish Museum

BERLIN, GERMANY

74 center and 75 *The museum, designed by the architect Daniel Libeskind and completed in 1998, is entirely clad with modular metal panels, placed one above the other and marked with jagged cuts that slash the walls, creating around 1500 irregularly shaped "windows."*

74 bottom *Libeskind based the plan of the building on a deconstructed and rearranged Star of David. The broken shape of the six-pointed star creates an intentionally angular structure, in which continuous symbolic references maintain a constant link between the architecture and the contents of the museum.*

Several important memorials to the Holocaust have been built in Berlin in recent years, including the Jewish Museum by designed by architect Daniel Libeskind and the Memorial to the Murdered Jews of Europe by Peter Eisenman. Daniel Libeskind's international fame is partly due to the commission that he won in 2003 in a prestigious competition for the re-design of another important place of memory, situated in the heart of New York: Ground Zero, the empty space left by the destruction of the World Trade Center. However, his most remarkable architectural work remains the Jewish Museum in Berlin, during 1998 and 1999 and opened in 2001.

Libeskind's project was successful precisely because his building was not conceived with the mere function of display, but instead devised and designed as though it were a great symbolic sculpture. It is in fact a highly evocative monument-museum, purposely aimed at arousing intense emotions in the visitor. The museum is situated on Lindenstrasse, and its intentionally angular structure makes the interior and surrounding space disoriented and irregular. One of the most interesting parts is the square Garden of Exile (originally known as the E.T.A. Hoffman Garden), marked off by a high reinforced

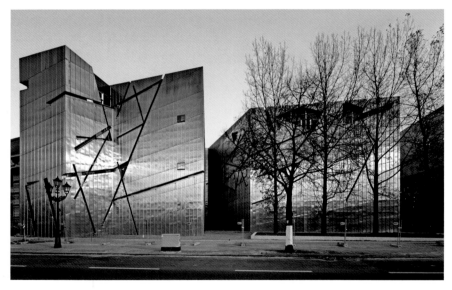

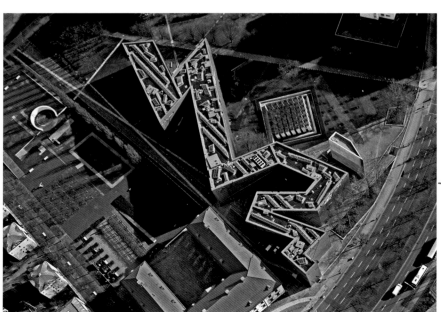

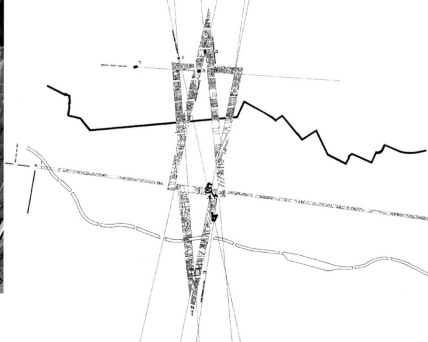

76-77 The museum has a display area of over 100,000 sq. ft (9290 sq. m) and the halls and corridors of the sections engage the visitor in a moving experience. With his work, Libeskind

76 bottom The rooms of the museum house both its permanent collection and temporary exhibitions, which concentrate mainly on investigating the 2000-year history of the German Jewish community. Personal possessions, photographs, documents and letters recounting the history of members of the community are displayed alongside objects and works of art that allow visitors to glean a deeper understanding of the immense Jewish culture.

77 The permanent collection is divided into 14 thematic sections that trace the history of Jewish culture in Germany from the Edict of Constantine, through the Middle Ages, until the present day.

Jewish Museum

concrete wall. Here, 49 square columns topped with olive trees, symbolizing a hope difficult to attain, commemorate the year of foundation of the state of Israel: '48, plus one that symbolically refers to the city of Berlin. The space between the columns creates a sort of maze, which generates a sensation of suffocation and the desire to escape, akin to that evoked by Peter Eisenman's memorial.

Libeskind based his design on the image of lightning bolt, an irregular zigzag line that forms the plan of the museum and is also repeated on the walls. This graphic symbol has a dual meaning: it is both the result of the deconstruction and rearrangement of the Star of David and an expression of laceration and cutting that is a metaphor for an extremely painful period in history. The entrance to the building is not

Another highly symbolic element, which also has a strong impact from outside, is the Holocaust memorial tower, defined by Libeskind as a "voided void," i.e. the vacuum and dramatic emptiness caused by the death of millions of people, which is also visually represented by a series of intentionally deserted rooms. The tower is reached by a black path marked by a wall, employed as a metaphor for the loss of reason, or light, that enabled such an abomination as the planned extermination of an entire people to come about. The oppressive sensation caused by the light that filters through the walls only through the cuts and jagged tears creates an atmosphere of disorientation and alteration in which the visitor is unable to see outside and feels almost suffocated and uneasy inside the museum. The exhibition

visible from the outside and is reached through the old museum, the Kollegienhaus, a 17th-century building rebuilt during the 1960s as the City Museum of Berlin. Once inside, visitors can choose from three possible paths, symbolizing the three different destinies of the Jews. That of the Holocaust crosses the path that leads to the garden – the symbol of exile – and that which leads to the stairs, representing the continuity and hope of the entire population. The Holocaust is thus presented as a dramatic moment that unites all Jews, even those who have not experienced it physically.

areas are arranged on three floors and also feature many symbolic architectural features that intentionally dramatize the space, such as the railroad tracks set into the floor, which are a highly evocative allusion to the mass deportations.

The permanent sections of the museum are home to documents and exhibits that illustrate the tragedy of the Holocaust: photographs, personal items documents, ceremonial objects, sculptures and paintings not only narrate the genocide that took place in the extermination camps, but also the age-old Jewish culture, its customs and its traditions.

78-79 The deconstructivist architecture of the Design Museum is just one of the elements of the Vitra architectural park in Weil am Rhein, which is an irresistible attraction for architecture buffs. The building was the first European work of Frank O. Gehry, one of the leading names in contemporary architecture.

79 Surprising overlapping volumes and outlines give a somewhat expressionist feel to Frank O. Gehry's building (1989).

Vitra Design Museum

WEIL AM RHEIN, GERMANY

The Vitra Design Museum is located in Weil am Rhein, a German town not far from the border with France and Switzerland and the Swiss city of Basel. It is named after a leading design company that produces famous chairs and furniture, of which it houses one of the most important and extensive collections in the world.

Outside the museum stands the monumental *Balancing Tools* sculpture by Claes Oldenburg and Coosje van Bruggen, while the central building of the complex – of which all components were designed by leading contemporary architects – is the work of Frank O. Gehry. It is surrounded by the other buildings of the Vitra factory complex, designed by Antonio Citterio, Nicholas Grimshaw and Alvaro Siza, the fire station by Zaha Hadid, and the conference pavilion by Tadao Ando. The original idea, which dates back to 1981, when Grimshaw was called to design a new factory after the previous one had been destroyed during a terrible fire, was to create a "collective identity" for the architecture, achieved through the presence on the same site of several different buildings able to attest to and

Vitra Design Museum

80 and 80-81 The Design Museum is itself both the highly conceptual product of design and its quintessential container, which takes visitors on an exciting tour of contemporary creativity. It is so popular that the number of visitors is constantly rising (reaching 80,000 in 2005) and plans have been made to extend the building. Vitra, a company that produces furniture by leading designers, established the museum in 1989 as an independent cultural institution.

offer the public an overview of the most diverse languages of contemporary architecture.

Following the construction of Grimshaw's design, the next part of the complex to be inaugurated was the Vitra Design Museum, in November 1989. This was the first European building designed by the famous Californian architect Frank O. Gehry and was a precursor of the sculptural power and plastic peculiarities of his later Guggenheim Museum in Bilbao. Indeed, for the first time in Europe Gehry created an architectural structure using geometric shapes that seem to explode disjointedly in space,

based on contrast between the parts rather than their harmony, giving rise to the sense of "frozen movement," as Gehry himself called it, which has become a distinctive feature of his work.

The museum's multiform sculptural quality derives from its ramps, towers and cubic volumes, which offer an internal display area of around 7500 sq. ft (700 sq. m) for the permanent collection and temporary exhibitions dedicated to the history of design and the most innovative and striking furniture. It is arranged on two floors, illuminated by the natural light that enters through large skylight-windows.

The building contrasts strongly with the nearby conference pavilion by Japanese architect Tadao Ando, in which anti-spectacularity and rapport with nature are expressed in terms of Oriental minimalism, and with Zaha Hadid's fire station that penetrates the space like a sharp blade, creating a sensation of vertigo and instability typical of the quest for movement that it shares with the work of Gehry and all the other architects of the deconstructivist movement. Deconstructivism is one of the most important movements of contemporary architecture and is often manifested in a contrasting rapport between the different, and sometimes apparently incongruous, parts of a building, and an openness to architecture that is never linear or static; it is motivated by an interest rather than by the quest for linear orderliness. In addition to Hadid and Gehry, the deconstructivist movement that has characterized the late 20th and early 21st centuries includes names such as Peter Einsenman, Bernard Tschumi, Daniel Libeskind and Coop Himmelblau, whose designs were displayed during the landmark "Deconstructivist Architecture" exhibition curated by Philip Johnson and held at the Museum of Modern Art, New York, in 1968.

82-83 This nocturnal view of the Mercedes-Benz Museum underscores the unusual effects created by the alternation of solids and voids.

82 bottom This sketch of the museum by its architect Ben van Berkel of UN Studio shows the main characteristic of the building, namely its display floors constituted by slightly sloping galleries formed by a reworked double spiral.

83 top During the design stage Van Berkel used digital software to rework the double spiral, derived from the famous Mercedes symbol.

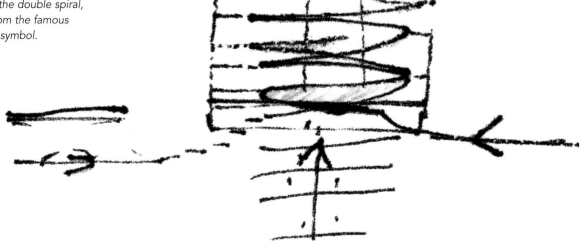

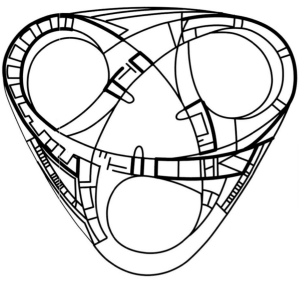

Mercedes-Benz Museum

STUTTGART, GERMANY

*83 bottom The cutaway model
of the museum shows the various
floors where some 175 vehicles
are displayed.*

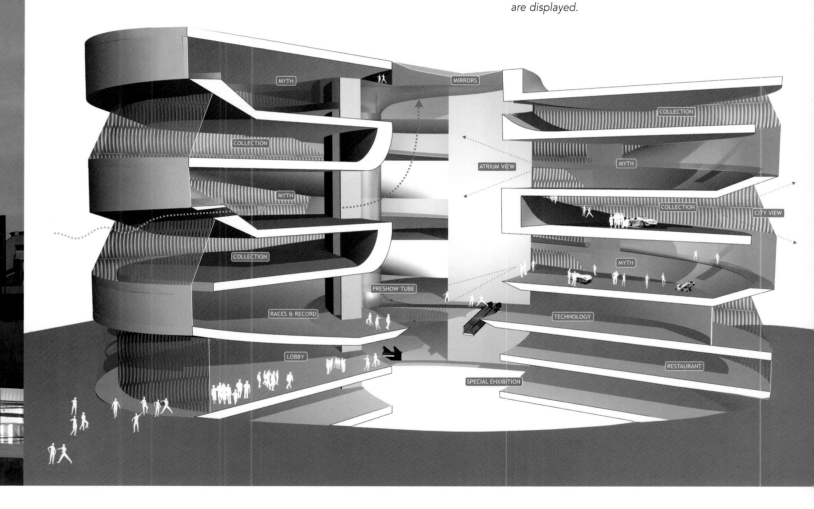

The Mercedes-Benz Museum in Stuttgart is housed in an imposing and innovative building that was designed to contain the collection of the world's oldest automobile manufacturer, formerly displayed in the Classic Center in Fellbach. Today's museum is a temple of the most advanced technology, which draws visitors from all over the world. Its spectacular appearance is heightened by its silver color, which is the symbol of the famous German manufacturer's racing cars.

The building is the work of architect Ben van Berkel, the director of UN Studio, whose winning project employed a digital design application that allowed him to mold the structure as though it were a sculpture. Berkel particularly admires the work of Bernini and Borromini and wished to create a sort of contemporary Baroque building by reworking a double spiral form, derived from the famous Mercedes symbol. After a three-year construction period, the museum was opened in May 2006. It is located at the Mercedes-Benz' headquarters in Stuttgart and is connected by an underground tunnel to the huge showroom where Mercedes-Benz displays all its models. The originality of the design is partly due to the complexity of the context in which it is set, which is heightened by the proximity of the freeway.

After entering the museum, visitors find themselves in a huge and imposing atrium. Here an elevator accompanies them to the third – top – floor where the exhibition commences, progressing down through the various, slightly sloping, levels.

84 top and left The interiors of the Mercedes-Benz Museum in Stuttgart have been designed to create an evocative combination of different levels that house display areas with special raised ramps for the cars.

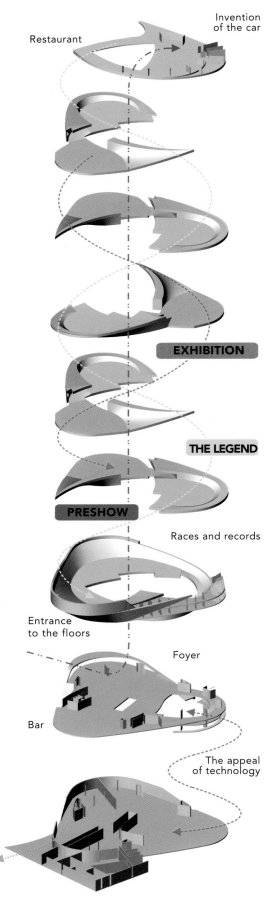

Restaurant

Invention of the car

EXHIBITION

THE LEGEND

PRESHOW

Races and records

Entrance to the floors

Foyer

Bar

The appeal of technology

Mercedes-Benz Museum

84 bottom The ramps presenting the most legendary cars are flanked by larger and brighter areas that display private vehicles, but also public ones – including buses, ambulances and military or industrial vehicles – arranged according to their construction date.

85 The Media Ring is a semi-open gallery that houses the Mercedes-Benz Legends display, presenting the manufacturer's most famous vehicles.

The display area totals covers 170,000 sq. ft (15,800 sq. m), where some 160 vehicles are arranged according to two main themes. The first of these is entitled "Legend," and is dedicated to the Mercedes-Benz legend. Its exhibits include both the most famous models and cars that once belonged to celebrity owners, including international stars like Sophia Loren, Princess Diana and Ringo Starr, and leading political figures, such as Kaiser Wilhelm II and Emperor Hirohito.

The other theme is "Collections" and features the vehicles produced during the 120 years of the brand's history, presented in chronological order. The two tours are independent, yet connected so that visitors can switch between them if they wish. Both routes end with the section entitled "Silver Arrows," which displays the most famous and successful Mercedes-Benz racing cars.

86 The architects of UN Studio fittingly chose silver as the main color of the Mercedes-Benz Museum – inside and out – because of its symbolic and evocative power, for it is a direct reference to the livery of many of the German manufacturer's historic racing cars.

87 top The museum displays a striking combination of industrial rationalism and Baroque style, echoing the intentions of its architect Ben van Berkel, an admirer of illustrious forerunners such as Gian Lorenzo Bernini.

Mercedes-Benz Museum

87 center History, advanced design and innovative technology are fundamental aspects of both the museum and Mercedes itself, and are masterly interpreted in van Berkel's architecture. Over a century of conceptual evolution is embodied in the museum's structures and itineraries, leaving the cars with the sole task of conveying the Mercedes legend.

87 bottom The sinuous, sculptural structure forms interiors with irregular, sloping walls, while the windows with steel struts afford views over Stuttgart's industrial area. A ring-shaped coffee bar is housed on the ground floor, from which a staircase leads to the display areas, guiding visitors with luminous trails.

This section features some 30 vehicles, past and present, and documents racing challenges that have inflamed the hearts and souls of numerous fans. The difference between the two paths is also underscored by the careful museum design: the Legend section is illuminated by artificial lighting designed to make the exhibition more theatrical and striking, while the Collection section is lit by large panoramic windows that form a pattern of solids and voids that is also visible on the exterior of the building.

Another important part of the exhibition illustrates interesting "behind-the-scenes" technical aspects. Indeed, the "Fascination of Technology" section displays the work and ongoing research of the Mercedes-Benz designers and engineers. It aims not only to offer an instructive explanation of technological development in the automobile industry of the past, but also draws on the most advanced technologies to provide suggestions and previews regarding what might be the innovative features of the automobiles of the future. In addition to the Gallery of Celebrities, there are also galleries divided up according vehicle type: the Gallery of Voyagers, Gallery of Carriers, Gallery of Helpers, and Gallery of Heroes. The museum layout is arranged to form a sort of journey through time that allows the gradual discovery of the vehicles, forms and technologies developed over the years by one of the most successful automobile manufacturers of all times.

Kunsthistorisches Museum
VIENNA, AUSTRIA

Vienna's Kunsthistorisches Museum, housed in a Neo-Classical building on the Ringstrasse, the city's smartest street, was commissioned by Emperor Francis Joseph in 1891. However, its eventful history commenced in 1363, when Rudolf IV, Duke of Austria, annexed the Tyrol and several works of medieval art passed to the Habsburg family. Later, Emperor Maximilian I (1459-1519), a particularly keen art collector, expanded this original nucleus. In 1567 Ferdinand II placed these early collections in Ambras Castle, near Innsbruck, along with others of armor and paintings, and a cabinet of curiosities featuring wondrous objects and marvels of natural history. Towards the end of the 16th century Archduke Ernst of Austria put together a collection including many very famous Flemish works, which

together one of the finest collections of paintings of all times. It not only featured works by Dutch and Flemish artists, but also examples of the German and Italian schools, including a famous bulk purchase of 16th-century Venetian paintings. When Leopold William resigned as governor in 1656, he moved to Vienna and installed his collection in the Hofburg Imperial Palace. The heir to the throne, Leopold I, was also an art lover, but his approach to collecting was more strongly influenced by social constraints and rank. During the 18th century, the gallery was merged with several collections belonging to the old imperial legacy and housed in the Stallburg. Although Emperor Charles VI (1685-1740) was not a great art expert, he ensured that the works were arranged in the most sumptuous and celebratory setting possible,

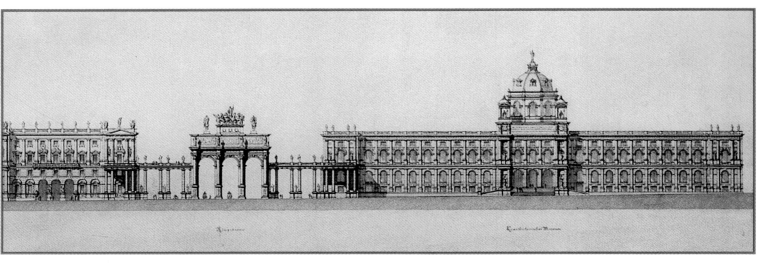

Karl, the son of Ferdinand II, subsequently sold to the Habsburg Emperor Rudolf II. By this time the emperor had already formed his own extraordinary art collection, featuring works by Dürer, Correggio and Bruegel, as well as a precious array of decorative and antique art. His collection too was a typical cabinet of curiosities, which also featured natural and artificial objects and marvels of all kinds. The emperor's great interest in collecting drove him to the relentless pursuit of every object that aroused his interest, and while this precious body of works increased his personal prestige, his true motivation was simply a deep and sincere love of art and culture.

The transition from assorted collections to a formal art gallery was brought about by Archduke Leopold William, Governor of the Spanish Netherlands, son of Ferdinand II and brother of Emperor Ferdinand III. The archduke was a great art lover and collector, and during the 17th century he put

according to Baroque taste, in the attempt to convey royal prestige and power to the few fortunate guests who had the honor of visiting the gallery.

An important stage in the history of the museum occurred during the rule of Emperor Joseph II (1747-1792), who transferred the imperial picture galleries to Belvedere Castle, where it was rearranged according to chronological criteria, reflecting the attempt to research and collate the artistic and historical background of the works. The emperor was also responsible for another important change. In 1781 it was finally decided to open the galleries to the public and for the first time the collections were considered from an educational and instructive viewpoint, rather than a simply private one aimed at celebrating imperial power. During the Napoleonic Wars the works were transferred to Vienna for fear of pillaging, and the collection was once again opened to the public in 1814-45.

88 In the original project, the Imperial Library was situated next to the left wing of the Kunsthistorisches Museum and the entire museum complex was joined to the Imperial Palace by a series of classical-style arches leading towards the Ringstrasse.

88-89 The main façade of the Kunsthistorisches Museum in Vienna overlooks the Ringstrasse and is positioned directly opposite the twin building of the Museum of Natural History. The museums were commissioned by Francis Joseph I and built between 1871 and 1891.

89 bottom The ceiling of the Main Staircase is decorated with a huge fresco of The Apotheosis of the Renaissance by Mihály von Munkácsy, who made around 150 preparatory sketches for the work.

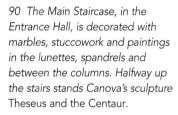

90 The Main Staircase, in the Entrance Hall, is decorated with marbles, stuccowork and paintings in the lunettes, spandrels and between the columns. Halfway up the stairs stands Canova's sculpture Theseus and the Centaur.

91 The octagonal Cupola Hall at the top of the Main Staircase is topped by a large dome decorated with reliefs and portrait medallions celebrating the most important patrons of the Habsburg family. The precious

materials of the décor include black and white marble, which is also echoed in the floor, while a circular opening in the dome provides natural light and alludes to the building's symbolic role as a Pantheon of art.

Kunsthistorisches Museum

Toward the mid 19th century, during the reign of Francis Joseph, the way of conceiving and enhancing the gallery took a new turn: the emperor ordered that the museum be coordinated by art historians, who were required to carry out research in the various sectors represented by the collections. In 1891 a new and exceptionally sumptuous building was especially designed and constructed to house the new collections. A "twin" building was also erected at the same time to house the Natural History Museum. The inauguration took place on October 17, 1891 with an official ceremony in Emperor Francis Josef's presence. Following the advent of World War I fall of the monarchy and the, the gallery became state property. From this time on the museum became a place increasingly accessible to all and dedicated to the service of the community.

During the 1930s it was necessary to restore and reorganize it, also due to developments in art-historical methodology that influenced the possible arrangements. A new layout was thus gradually devised in which the individual artists became less important, and greater attention was paid to the collection of works as a whole, abandoning hierarchical divisions between so-called "major" and "minor" artists. During World War II, several of the collections were placed in the Altausee salt mines for protection. However, the Kunsthistorisches Museum suffered serious structural damage, preventing the return of the works after the war ended and forcing the museum to stage loan exhibitions throughout Europe while the Kunsthistorisches was restored. The building work was completed in the 1950s.

The Kunsthistorisches is home to countless famous works, including The Crucifixion by Rogier van der Weyden, St. Sebastian by Andrea Mantegna, Hans Memling's triptych featuring the Virgin and Child Enthroned, the Madonna in the Meadow by Raphael, The Three Philosophers and Laura by Giorgione, the Young Man against a White Curtain by Lorenzo Lotto, Parmigianino's Self-Portrait, Benvenuto Cellini's Saliera, Susanna and the Elders by Tintoretto, The Tower of Babel by Pieter Bruegel the Elder, and many other masterpieces by Veronese, Titian, Correggio, Guercino, Rubens and Poussin.

Veuë du Palais Royal

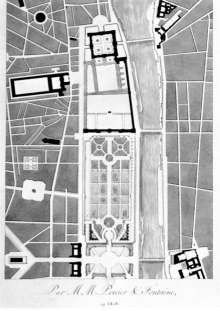

Par M.M. Percier & Fontaine.

Louvre Museum

PARIS, FRANCE

The architectural history of the Louvre Palace is much longer than that of the actual museum. Indeed, it originated as a 12th-century fortress built by King Philip Augustus on a site that then formed the western boundary of Paris. The complex began to resemble a true palace between the 14th and 15th centuries, under three of the most influential kings in French history: Charles V, Francis I (who razed the medieval castle)

and Henry IV (who commissioned the Grande Galerie that runs along the Seine between the Louvre and the Tuileries. Major additions were made to the palace over the centuries and Napoleon III added the Denon wing on the Seine side, opposite the Richelieu wing, forming a huge complex with the Tuileries Palace, which was burned to the ground in 1871 following the collapse of the Second Empire. However, the art collections survived the upheaval and today the Louvre is one of the world's greatest museums, due not only to the size and richness of its collections, but also to its fundamental role in the history of the museum as a modern institution devoted to the conservation and

transmission of culture. Although the intention to transform the palace housing the royal collections into a museum open to all had already been expressed following a debate held during the final years of the *ancien régime* under Louis XVI, the Louvre did not open to the public until August 10, 1793, on the first anniversary of the Republic. It was a symbol of the conquests of the Revolution, and as such was established with the intention of becoming a democratic instrument of education and knowledge available to every citizen.

In 1794 a management committee known as the Conservatoire was founded to establish procedures for selecting and exhibiting the collections in order to ensure that the revolutionary principles were respected, and it was even decided to put what were regarded as "unsuitable" works for the particular cultural climate into storage. In 1799 the establishment formerly known as the Musée Français was renamed the Musée Central des Arts, becoming the Musée Napoléon in 1803. In 1806 Napoleon himself commissioned the architects Percier and Fontaine to extend the North Wing on the Rue Rivoli, with the intention of expanding both the building and the collections. The Napoleonic period was a vitally important time for the expansion of the collections. During this period the Louvre, like many other leading European museums, was enriched with works plundered by the Napoleonic troops, which included extraordinary masterpieces. During the Bourbon Restoration the museum was forced to return many of these works, and thus commenced a campaign of acquisitions with the aim of building collections representative of the art of all periods and genres.

The nature of the collections thus became increasingly varied and the gaps constituted by periods formerly not represented – such as Greek, Roman, Etruscan and Oriental antiquity – were gradually filled.

92 top left This 19th-century engraving shows the sumptuous Royal Palace that opened its doors to the public as a museum in 1793. The *construction of the historic residence of the French kings, originally designed as a fortress, commenced as early as the 12th century.*

92 top right The Galerie Napoléon on the Rue de Rivoli was built between 1802 and 1812 to connect the Louvre to the Tuileries. It was *commissioned by Napoleon himself from architects Charles Percier (1764–1838) and Pierre-François-Léonard Fontaine (1762–1853).*

92 bottom and 92-93 The Louvre as we know it today gradually took shape over a period of around 800 years, expanding along the right bank of the Seine. Numerous changes, both decorative and architectural, have been made since the Middle Ages, bearing witness to the stratified development of the complex, while preserving the unity of the building.

93 bottom Like its ancient Egyptian forerunners, the Louvre Pyramid in the Cour Napoléon is surrounded by three smaller pyramids. The dimensions of the central structure are proportional to those of the Great Pyramid at Giza. The structure has generated much controversy and has had great public impact, especially in Paris.

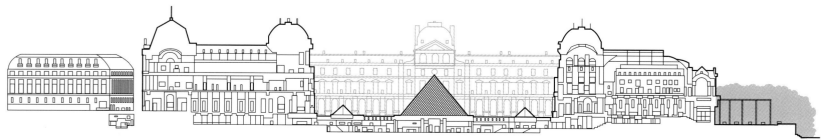

Louvre Museum

Napoleon III entrusted Louis Visconti and subsequently Hector Lefuel to extend the palace, demolishing the neighborhood that separated the two wings, in the center of which the new Cour Napoléon was built. Following the fire of 1871, which destroyed the adjacent Tuileries Palace, an important reconstruction project was completed in 1882. In 1948 the Louvre exchanged several of its archaeological collections with the Musée Guimet, acquiring important works of ancient Egyptian art in return. The 1980's marked another important stage in the history of the Louvre, with the launch of the "Grand Louvre" renovation project. This was just one of the great building projects commissioned for Paris by the French president François Mitterrand, along with others such as the new French National Library, the Opéra Bastille and the great Arche de la Défense.

94-95 The entrance of the Louvre, characterized by I.M. Pei's 70-ft (21-m) glass pyramid with steel framework, rests on a dark granite base and was built as part of the "Grand Louvre" project.

94 bottom Ieoh Ming Pei's "Grand Louvre" extension project for the museum was discussed during the Arcachon seminar in 1984. The work was divided into two stages, the first of which

involved the Cour Napoléon, the construction of the entrance Pyramid (visibile at the center of this longitudinal section), and the Carrousel Garden, which was completed in 1989.

95 The entrance pyramid leads down to the underground foyer, also designed by I.M. Pei, which allows access to the museum's three main wings, known as the Denon, Sully and Richelieu wings.

Louvre Museum

96-97 The reception hall beneath the Cour Napoléon is flooded with light, which enters through the glass walls of the pyramid overhead. The expansion and modernization of the museum, including the construction of the pyramid, was commissioned by French president François Mitterrand.

97 An urban myth maintains that the number of panes of glass forming the faces of the pyramid is 666, a number with esoteric connotations. Actually there are seven more panes, for a total of 673, connected by over 100 tons of metal cables, kept in tension by the weight of the glass.

98-99 *The Salle des Cariatides, designed by architect Pierre Lescot, is named after the caryatids supporting the tribune that housed the orchestra when the room was used for feasts and banquets. Today it is home to the museum's collection of Greek and Roman statuary, including the famous Diana of Versailles.*

98 bottom *The Louvre's collection of Assyrian art comes mainly from the archaeological digs commenced in the mid 19th century. The famous finds of the Khorsabad excavations are now housed in the Cour Khorsabad, in the Richelieu wing.*

Louvre Museum

The symbol of this phase of expansion and modernization of the museum is the famous new entrance, characterized by the pyramid designed by architect I.M. Pei, situated in the center of the Cour Napoléon and surrounded by imposing fountains. The opening of the pyramid in 1989 was followed by that of the Richelieu wing in 1993, and in 1997 the Louvre finally reopened to the public with an extra 108,000 feet of exhibition

99 top right The ancient Greek statue of Aphrodite known as the Venus de Milo is one of the Louvre's most famous works. Carved about 100 BC and found on the island of Melos in 1820, it has subsequently become one of the symbols of the perfection of classical art.

99 top left The Winged Victory of Samothrace (ca 190 BC) was found in 1863 by the French archaeologist Charles Champoiseau on the Aegean island of Samothrace. The figure originally held a trumpet and was designed to stand on the prow of a ship.

space in the oldest parts of the palace, along the Seine (Denon wing) and around the square courtyard (Sully wing). In 1999 a further 54,000 square feet were added.

Arranged on four floors and divided into the three Richelieu, Sully and Denon wings, the Louvre houses important works of art and archaeological exhibits that span the entire history of mankind, from the ancient civilizations through to the Middle Ages and the Renaissance, until reaching the French art of the 19th century.

99 bottom Several sculptures from the gardens of Marly-le-Châtel, the residence of Louis XIV situated west of Paris, are displayed in the Cour Marly, in the Richelieu wing. This area, along with the Cour Puget, was part of the "Grand Louvre" project directed by I.M. Pei.

100 top The Grand Galerie connects the Louvre and the Tuileries. It was commenced in 1595 under Henry IV and completed in 1610. Louis XVI commissioned Hubert Robert to convert it into a Royal Museum, and when the Louvre was opened it was used to house collections of paintings and sculpture.

100 bottom left The Salons Napoléon III, including the magnificent Grand Salon, are situated in the Richelieu wing and were built between 1852 and 1860, under the direction of Hector-Martin Lefuel.

100 bottom right The Galerie d'Apollon in the Denon wing of the Louvre was commenced under Charles IX in the 16th century, but was destroyed by fire and rebuilt by the architect Louis Le Vau during the 17th century. The painter Charles Le Brun was commissioned to decorate it with an iconographic theme in which Louis XIV, the Sun King, was identified with Apollo.

101 One of the galleries displaying the museum's collection of Roman statuary is housed in the former summer apartments of Anne of Austria, the mother of the future Roi Soleil, Louis XIV, which were decorated by Francesco Romanelli during the mid 17th century.

Louvre Museum

The museum's many large halls thus allow the visitor to trace the history of the succession of important civilizations that developed from India to the Mediterranean from Neolithic times. They are home to extremely important works of ancient Greek and Roman art, including the *Venus de Milo* and the *Winged Victory of Samothrace*, extensive sections dedicated to Sumerian, Assyrian and Babylonian antiquities, and precious archaeological finds from the Iranian Plateau and the eastern borders of Iran. The museum boasts a particularly rich collection of Egyptian antiquities, which dates back to the period of the Bourbon Restoration. It presents a picture of everyday life, with exhibits arranged in thematic and chronological order in rooms dedicated to the activities or types of houses of ancient Egypt, and historical information regarding the artistic development of this culture and its religious characteristics and symbols.

Centre Pompidou

PARIS, FRANCE

The Centre Pompidou (the Beaubourg) is situated in the heart of Paris between the Les Halles and Marais districts. It was the brainchild of Président Georges Pompidou, who in 1969 proposed to build a museum center dedicated to all forms of contemporary art in the capital. The decision to establish a museum of contemporary art also stemmed from the need for a larger and more suitable home for the 20th-century collections that were formerly housed in other important Parisian galleries, such as the Luxembourg, Jeu de Paume and Palais de Tokyo. The Centre Pompidou was thus founded as the ideal continuation of the collections of the Louvre and Orsay museums, and the model adopted for its design – in terms of both structure and organization of the cultural institutions that it houses – immediately became the symbol of the museum as a site of cultural production, where exhibitions are not merely shows to be visited passively, but also occasions to engage visitors as actively as possible. Indeed, the Centre Pompidou is not only a museum, but also home to the BPI (Public Information Library), MNAM (Museum of Modern Art), CCI (Center for Industrial Creation) and a series of structures dedicated to various kinds of recreational and cultural activities, such as the publishing department that produces books, periodicals and audio-video materials, the children's workshop and the Cinémathèque, which hosts meetings and conferences.

The Centre Pompidou's self-styled image as a "cultural machine," whose workings are its various departments, is also effectively expressed in its architecture. The building, designed by Richard Rogers and Renzo Piano and constructed between 1971 and 1978, has a steel structure whose façade exposes, rather than hides, its constituent parts. The series of pipes, ducts and structural elements visible on the exterior are colored according to their function: air ducts are blue, water pipes are green, electricity lines are yellow, and elevator cables and emergency exits are red.

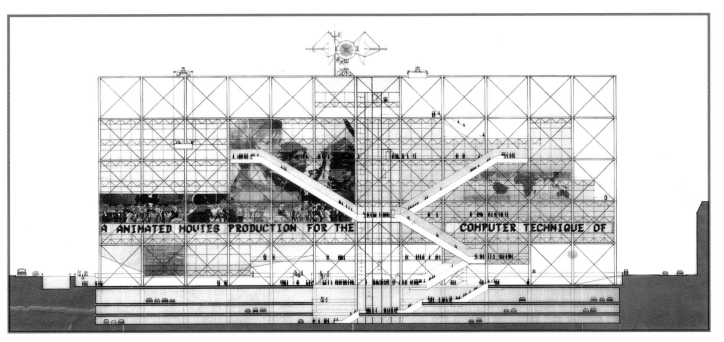

102 top This drawing shows one of the early stages of the project designed by Richard Rogers and Renzo Piano, whose intention was that of creating a sort of "cultural production machine."

102 bottom The key to the success of the design presented for the competition was its transparency. Indeed, the flow of visitors inside the building can be seen from outside, moving in elevators in transparent tubes and past the huge glazed surfaces.

102-103 The Centre Pompidou, shown here in an aerial view that emphasizes its compact volumes and striking appearance, was built between 1971 and 1978 in the Les Halles district of Paris and almost immediately became one of the city's most popular attractions.

103 bottom As can be seen in this view from the Rue de Renard, the ducts and structural components of the building are not hidden behind a façade, but are instead intentionally exposed and colored according to their function: air ducts are blue, water pipes are green, and elevator cables and emergency exits are red.

104 top and 104-105 The escalators serving the various floors of the Centre Pompidou and the walkways running along the length of each level are housed inside evocative transparent tubes, allowing the constant flow of visitors to be seen from outside and affording spectacular views of the city to those inside.

104 center The huge entrance hall introduces visitors to the system of signs used to mark the floors housing the permanent collection and the temporary exhibitions.

104 bottom The Flammarion Bookshop is one of the features of this extraordinary "cultural machine." Indeed, the Centre Pompidou was designed not only as an exhibition space, but also as an active and multipurpose cultural center, with an array of facilities, such as a library, a cinema and areas for educational activities.

Centre Pompidou

Since its inauguration on January 31, 1977, the Centre Pompidou has become one of the world's most famous and most visited museums. Part of its collections were actually already housed in Paris: the National Museum of Modern Art was formerly located in the Palais de Tokyo, whose first Director, Jean Cassou, added to the important masterpieces inherited from the Luxembourg Museum with works by Picasso, Braque Matisse, Chagall and Brancusi donated by the artists themselves. Other incredibly important works were acquired through the donations of entire private collections, such as that

of Daniel Cordier, dedicated to *art brut* and Dubuffet, and those of Louise and Michel Leiris, comprising mainly Cubist works. The policy of acquisitions conducted by the museum, and in some cases funded by private benefactors, has further enriched the collection with Neo-plastic works and pieces by 21st-century artists such as Mike Kelley and Tony Oursler.

The Centre Pompidou currently houses almost 53,000 works and boasts one of the most important collections of 20th-century art in the world, which documents the artistic transformations of the last century through painting, sculpture,

LIVE AND DIE
DIE AND DIE
SHIT AND DIE
PISS AND DIE
EAT AND DIE
SLEEP AND DIE
LOVE AND DIE
HATE AND DIE
FUCK AND DIE
SPEAK AND DIE
LIE AND DIE
HEAR AND DIE
CRY AND DIE
KISS AND DIE
RAGE AND DIE
LAUGH AND DIE
TOUCH AND DIE
FEEL AND DIE
FEAR AND DIE
SICK AND DIE
WELL AND DIE
BLACK AND DIE
WHITE AND DIE
YELLOW AND DIE
LIVE AND LIVE
DIE AND LIVE
SHIT AND LIVE
PISS AND LIVE
EAT AND LIVE
SLEEP AND LIVE
LOVE AND LIVE
HATE AND LIVE
FUCK AND LIVE
SPEAK AND LIVE
LIE AND LIVE
HEAR AND LIVE
CRY AND LIVE
KISS AND LIVE
RAGE AND LIVE
LAUGH AND LIVE
TOUCH AND LIVE
FEEL AND LIVE
FEAR AND LIVE
SICK AND LIVE
WELL AND LIVE
BLACK AND LIVE
WHITE AND LIVE
YELLOW AND LIVE
SING AND DIE
SCREAM AND DIE
YOUNG AND DIE
OLD AND DIE
CUT AND DIE
RUN AND DIE
STAY AND DIE
PLAY AND DIE
KILL AND DIE
SUCK AND DIE
COME AND DIE
GO AND DIE
KNOW AND DIE
TELL AND DIE
SMELL AND DIE
FALL AND DIE
RISE AND DIE
STAND AND DIE
SIT AND DIE
SPIT AND DIE
TRY AND DIE
FAIL AND DIE
SMILE AND DIE
THINK AND DIE
PAY AND DIE
SING AND LIVE
SCREAM AND LIVE
YOUNG AND LIVE
OLD AND LIVE
CUT AND LIVE
RUN AND LIVE
STAY AND LIVE
PLAY AND LIVE
KILL AND LIVE
SUCK AND LIVE
COME AND LIVE
GO AND LIVE
KNOW AND LIVE
TELL AND LIVE
SMELL AND LIVE
FALL AND LIVE
RISE AND LIVE
STAND AND LIVE
SIT AND LIVE
SPIT AND LIVE
TRY AND LIVE
FAIL AND LIVE
SMILE AND LIVE
THINK AND LIVE
PAY AND LIVE

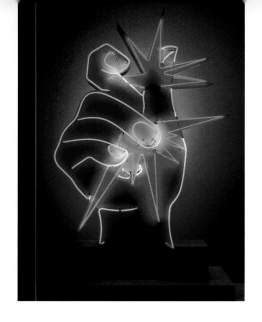

106 This work by Bruce Nauman is entitled One Hundred Live and Die and testifies to the concerns of the artist and conceptual art in general, which concentrates on the use of language and all forms of communication.

107 top The bright neon-lighting America America (1964) is a work by Martial Raysse, the French artist associated with the 1960s Nouveau Réalisme movement that questioned the perceptive approach to reality by using industrial and recycled materials and a neo-Dadaist language.

107 bottom The museum's large rooms dedicated to modern and contemporary art are able to accommodate huge installations, such as the hypnotic work of Israeli optical-kinetic artist Yaacov Agam, which creates optical effects that alter the spectator's visual perception.

Centre Pompidou

architecture, film, new media, photography and design. Two of the building's seven floors are entirely dedicated to the display of these works: the fourth floor covers a period stretching from the art of the 1960s to the present day, with works by important artists such as Giuseppe Penone, Christian Boltanski, Joseph Beuys, Donald Judd and Richard Serra. The fifth floor presents a chronological display of works stretching back in time from the 1960s to the beginning of the 20th century, and monographic rooms concentrating on the leading artists of the last century, with Pablo Picasso's paintings and sculpture, Jackson Pollock's action painting, Marcel Duchamp's ready-made, Alexander Calder's mobiles, and Joan Miró's paintings.

In addition to the permanent collections, each year the Centre Pompidou organizes temporary exhibitions dedicated to important 20th-century artists or to wider themes of interest relevant to the study of modern and contemporary art.

The Centre Pompidou is not merely a cultural institution. Indeed, the large and evocative square on which it stands has become a favorite meeting place for tourists and locals alike and an open-air stage for the continuous performances and shows of street artists. The adjoining Place Stravinsky is adorned with a spectacular dynamic fountain designed by the Swiss and French sculptors Jean Tinguely and Niki de Saint-Phalle, which further symbolizes the 20th-century works housed in the Centre.

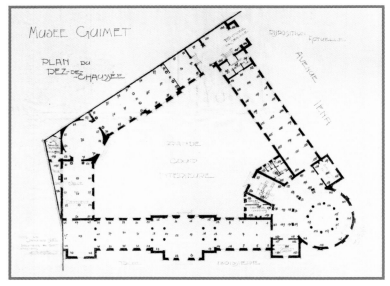

Musée Guimet

PARIS, FRANCE

The Musée Guimet was the brainchild of Émile Guimet (1836-1918), a Lyons industrialist with a passion for the religion of ancient Egypt and for ancient Oriental history. Guimet had always dreamed of opening an institution dedicated to these themes. He managed to make his dream come true in 1879, when he opened a museum in his hometown. Here he displayed the works of art that he had bought and collected during his extensive travels in Greece, Egypt, Japan, China and India. The collections were subsequently transferred to the museum in Paris that bears his name, which was opened in 1889.

The opening of the Musée Guimet was due in part to growing public interest in Oriental history and culture. Indeed, during this period great finds and discoveries had been made by major archaeological expeditions, such as those led by Louis Delaporte in Siam and Cambodia – which uncovered a large part of the museum's current collection of Khmer art – Charles Varat in Korea, and Jacques Bacot in Tibet. Over the years, part of the finds of these and other expeditions ended up in the Guimet collection.

In 1927 a significant change occurred, as the museum came under the administrative control of the French museums network and extended its collections further with new research and excavation campaigns led by Paul Pelliot and Édouard Chavannes in Central Asia and China.

During the first half of the 20th century the museum also acquired precious Southeast Asian works of art, formerly displayed at the Trocadéro Museum, and Oriental pieces from the Louvre in exchange for its Egyptian section. During the 1950s and 1960s the Musée Guimet became one of the world's leading museums of Asian art, and gradually expanded under a series of directors who developed and enhanced its various sections according to their own backgrounds and interests. The great scholar Philippe Stern developed the museum's research activities, its library and, above all, its photographic archives. These areas of the museum, which are still accessible to visitors, were also enhanced by his successor, Jeannine Auboyer, who was responsible for the renovation and extension of the building carried out in the 1960s and 1970s.

The 1990s were also marked by innovative changes. The first of these came in 1991, when the Buddhist Pantheon, displaying a selection of the original collections brought back

108-109 The photograph shows the general layout of the building, dating from the second half of the 19th century. The main roads of Georges Haussmann's urban redevelopment plan are particularly visible.

108 bottom left The old library of the Musée Guimet has a glass dome with a gallery adorned with Neoclassical statues like those

embellishing the building's façade. The library houses over 100,000 precious books on ancient Asian art and archaeology.

108 bottom right A plan of the building, dated 1937, reveals its irregular perimeter, caused by the acute angle of the junction of Rue Hamelin and Rue d'Iéna, which run to the left and right of the rotunda that houses the library.

from Japan by Émile Guimet, was opened in an annex of the museum in collaboration with Bernard Frank of the Collège de France. The final stage in the renovation of the museum was carried out between 1993 and 1996. The architects Henri and Bruno Gaudin reorganized its display areas and layouts, dividing up the sections housed on the four floors of the building according to the geographical area of origin of the exhibits, in order to make it easier for even the uninitiated visitor to understand the collections.

The museum's largest collection is that of Chinese art, composed of over 20,000 items and featuring splendid jade and pottery pieces from the Neolithic period, bronzes from the Shang and Zhou dynasties, Buddhist sculptures – some of which are displayed in the evocative setting of the Pantheon – *mingqi*

figures from Han and Tang tombs, and an extraordinary variety of pottery, celadonware and porcelain, as well as a selection of lacquered and rosewood ornaments and around 100 paintings spanning the period between the Tang and the Qing dynasties. The section dedicated to Southeast Asian art is equally comprehensive and extraordinary, comprising a series of sculptures from the Champa kingdom that bear witness to the fusion of the various cultures of the area, also known as "Indianized Vietnam," and exhibits from Cambodia, including the famous 7th-century head of King Jayavarman.

The rooms dedicated to Central Asia (also known as Serindia) are home to unique Buddhist manuscripts and a series of exhibits from the leading Buddhist centers that originally developed as stopping places for the caravans that traveled along the Silk Road.

Musée Guimet

110-111 The Khmer art room of the Musée Guimet houses a collection of ancient Southeast Asian art formed by the merging of the museum's old collection, pieced together by Étienne Aymonier, with that of the Trocadéro Indo-Chinese Museum, founded and curated by Louis Delaporte. The photograph shows statues of kings and heads of gods (Brahma in particular) and friezes from Angkor Wat, in Cambodia.

111 A frieze of nagas (semi-divine beings, half human and half serpentine, with a protective role) from the temple complex of Angkor Wat is appropriately positioned at the foot of the museum's staircase, thus symbolically maintaining its original function.

The sculptures from the Gandhara region of Afghanistan and Pakistan, which include the famous "Foucher" Bodhisattva, constitute the earliest examples of Buddhist iconography and are of utmost importance. Other sections are dedicated to the collections of Himalayan art, including Nepalese and Tibetan thang-ka and bronzes; Indian art, featuring bronzes, earthenware and wooden sculptures; and Korean art.

The evocative and instructive layout of the Musée Guimet not only offers visitors a detailed look at ancient Oriental history, but also an insight into the history of Western archaeology whose expeditions and excavations allowed these extraordinary collections illustrating distant, and what were then little-known, lands to be assembled.

112-113 The Gare d'Orsay, inaugurated on 14 July 1900, was designed by Victor Laloux. The building featured a metal frame with a stone façade that blended with the city's historic buildings, such as the Louvre. The project of the ACT architecture group features a series of levels and steps along the central hall and on the raised terraces on the sides, thus enhancing the sculptures illuminated by the restored lamps designed by Laloux and the natural light that filters through the glazed roof.

113 A color analysis study was carried out for the interiors, in order to achieve shades as close as possible to the original hues for the stuccowork, decoration and metal structures. The winning design by the ACT architecture group, composed of Jean-Paul Philippon, Renaud Bardon and Pierre Colboc, reversed the original layout of the station, adding an entrance on the Rue de Bellechasse, visible in this cross-section of the building (bottom).

Musée d'Orsay

PARIS, FRANCE

The Musée d'Orsay is one of the most important, evocative and historical museums in Paris. In 1897 the Orléans railroad company decided to build a station in the heart of the French capital, a stone's throw from the Tuileries, on the bank of the Seine, not far from the Louvre. In an attempt to reassure the local inhabitants, worried about the construction of an industrial building that they feared would disfigure their handsome district, the company called for designs from three famous architects: Victor Laloux, Emile Bénard and Lucien Magne. The winning design was that by Laloux, which

by important artists commissioned by Laloux. The Gare d'Orsay thus successfully blended with its historic neighbors and at the same time represented a synthesis of modern, turn-of-the-century architecture. However, the building was progressively abandoned and in 1939 was completely closed to long-distance trains.

The station's transformation into a museum came during the 1970s, but not before it had been used for a series of different purposes, including a parcel sorting center during World War II, a set for Orson Welles' famous movie *The Trial*, the headquarters of the Renaud-Barrault theatrical company, and finally as a

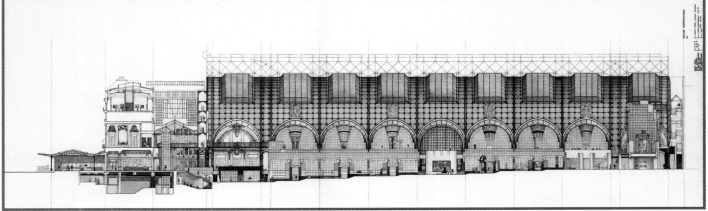

featured a great hall running the whole length of the building, topped by an imposing slate-tiled mansard roof. Construction commenced on the site of the burnt ruins of the Palais d'Orsay, and the station was opened on July 14, 1900, on occasion of the World Fair.

The glass and steel building was 105 ft (32 m) tall with an imposing stone façade, and also had a huge, luxurious hotel. The innovative, non-polluting electric trains allowed even the interior of the station to be richly decorated with stuccowork and frescoes

temporary auction house. In 1975 the Direction des Musées de France proposed the establishment of a museum to house several important collections dedicated mainly – but not exclusively – to the Impressionist movement. Many of these came from large private donations, including the Moreau-Nélaton collection, containing works from the Romantic and Impressionist periods; the Alfred Chauchard bequest, focusing on the Barbizon school; and the Édouard Mollard collection, comprising a series of 19th-century landscapes.

114 The lamps that hang from the high, vaulted ceiling and the large, majestic clock that dominates the central hall of the Musée d'Orsay are features from the building's previous life as a station.

114-115 The huge clock reminds visitors to the Musée d'Orsay of the building's former role as a station. It is visible both outside, on the Rue de Bellechasse, and inside, in what was once the station's grand hotel and is now the museum's café-restaurant.

116-117 The Impressionist Gallery is housed inside the roof, which Laloux designed to echo the structure of the Louvre, across the Seine. The glazing allows zenithal lighting and the walls are made from plastered steel.

117 top Many priceless works of late 19th-century French art are displayed in the rooms of the Impressionist Gallery. One of these is dedicated to the paintings and sculptures of Edgar Degas, featuring his famous ballet dancers.

117 bottom The first three Salons Ovales, in which the original domes designed by Victor Laloux have been preserved, house an exhibition of the pictorial movements documenting the transition

from Naturalism to Symbolism (featuring works by Bonnard, Denis, Klimt, Munch, Roussel), while the other three Salons, whose structure has been partly modified, are dedicated to the applied arts and Art Nouveau.

Musée d'Orsay

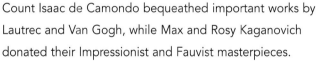

Count Isaac de Camondo bequeathed important works by Lautrec and Van Gogh, while Max and Rosy Kaganovich donated their Impressionist and Fauvist masterpieces.

Before entering the Musée d'Orsay collections, some of these works, lacking a single permanent home, were displayed in the Musée du Luxembourg, which exhibited the works of living artists from 1818 to 1939; the Louvre; the Galerie Nationale du Jeu de Paume; and the National Museum of Modern Art. The Musée d'Orsay was thus founded to bridge the gap between the older artistic exhibits displayed in the Louvre and the contemporary art of the Centre Pompidou.

In 1978 a competition was held for the restoration of the Orsay building. The ACT architecture group, composed of Jean-Paul Philippon, Renaud Bardon and Pierre Colboc, were the winners. In 1980 a second competition was announced, this time for the design of the interiors, which was won by the Italian architect Gae Aulenti. The exhibition space of the museum, which Président François Mitterrand officially

opened on December 1, 1986 by, is arranged on three levels that still reveal aspects of the building's original function.

The extraordinary works displayed in the rooms of this splendid museum include priceless masterpieces that have made the Musée d'Orsay world famous, including Édouard Manet's *Le Déjeuner sur l'Herbe* and *Olympia*, and Gustave Courbet's *Origin of the World*, Edgar Degas' famous ballet dancers, Pierre-Auguste Renoir's dancers, and works by other great masters, including Jean-Auguste-Dominique Ingres, Vincent van Gogh, Paul Cézanne, Paul Gauguin, Claude Monet, Henri Rousseau and Henri de Toulouse-Lautrec. The sculpture gallery features works by Auguste Rodin, Aristide Maillol and Antoine Bourdelle. However, the museum's multidisciplinary approach is also evident in the rich array of exhibits regarding the fields of architecture, graphics, photography and decorative arts, which illustrate the historical and architectural changes that, from 1948, led to the dawn of a second modernity: that of the avant-garde movements.

Musée d'Orsay

118-119 The Gare d'Orsay also had a luxurious hotel, complete with a richly adorned Salle des Fêtes. The old dance hall is situated beneath the fifth floor of the building, where is housed the Café des Hauteurs, while the museum's bookshop is located on the ground floor.

119 top The Salle à Manger Charpentier is housed on an intermediate floor dedicated to the applied arts. It is a dining room dating from the turn of the 20th century, decorated by Alexandre Charpentier for the Champrosay home of the banker Adrien Bénard.

119 bottom The Salons Ovales dedicated to the Art Nouveau style display period furniture, including the Majorelle chairs, dating from around 1902–1909, and the mahogany chairs by Henry van de Velde (visible in the foreground of the photograph) from the end of the 19th century.

Musée du Quai Branly

PARIS, FRANCE

The Musée du Quai Branly, one of Paris' newest museums, is situated on the left bank of the Seine, at the foot of the Eiffel Tower. It is not merely a museum, but also a research and study center, inaugurated on 22 June 2006 in the large and versatile building designed by French architect Jean Nouvel, who won the design competition held in 1999. The museum is devoted to the display and promotion of non-Western art and culture. Nouvel, who is particularly well known and esteemed in Paris as the designer of the Institut du Monde Arabe and the Cartier Foundation for Contemporary Art, has created a structure that covers an area of around 430,000 sq. ft (40,000 sq. m), consisting of four asymmetrically arranged buildings, where natural elements such as light and greenery play a particularly important role. Before starting to discover the exotic stories that the museum's exhibits recount, the visitor is invited to explore the building's exterior, which reveals itself gradually to the eye. The museum is set among thick greenery, planned by botanist Patrick Blanc, which partially hides it from view.

120-121 As part of the structure is deliberately hidden by the complex layout, an aerial view is the best way to admire the arrangement of Jean Nouvel's project. The photograph shows the actual museum marked by the trapezoidal area in the center, while the darker square to its right is the institute's research and study center. The oval on the left marks the location of the service structures of the complex.

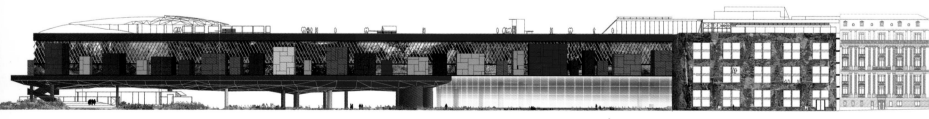

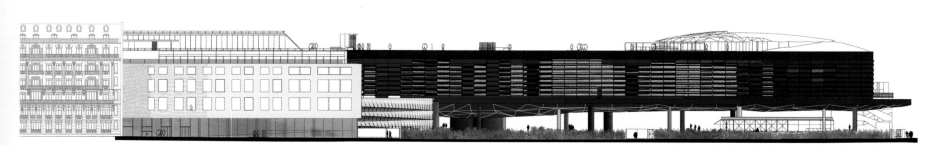

120 bottom Two schematic views show the north façade (top) and south façade. The former, uniquely characterized by a series of colored "boxes," overlooks the Seine.

121 bottom Although it covers an area of around 430,000 sq. ft (40,000 sq. m), less than half the land belonging to the museum is actually occupied by buildings. Indeed, the greenery is as important as the architecture, which it complements.

122 The "Mur Végétal" devised by Patrick Blanc covers an area of over 8600 sq. ft (800 sq. m) and has been described as "impressive." The thick greenery is composed of 15,000 plants of 150 different species. This living wall covers the outside of the Branly building, which houses the museum's offices.

123 top left The apparent – and surprising – precariousness of the colored "boxes" is derived from the need to separate the contents of the museum. Each of them houses objects regarding a particular people or culture, while others are dedicated to their musical traditions.

123 top right and bottom The various stories of the museums are connected by a long spiral ramp that resembles a giant snail. The concept of "passage" played a fundamental role in the design of the museum itself, which was envisaged as a sort of intercultural bridge.

123 center These two views of the north and south façades emphasize the position of the central structure – built on piles to reinforce the conceptual analogy with a bridge – and a section of the huge window of the complex, which constitutes another fundamental feature of the design.

Musée du Quai Branly

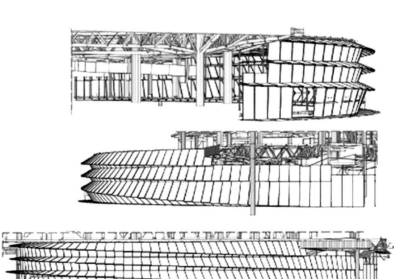

To reach it the visitor must cross a lush garden, which creates a deliberately wild and untamed effect. The surrounding garden, which covers a huge area of over 170,000 sq. ft (15,800 sq. m), was planned by landscape gardener Gilles Clément, while the central structure of the building perches on piles above this "forest."

From the outside of the building some or so 20 colored boxes seem to perch precariously on its walls, as though suspended, while the wall that runs along the Seine for about 650 ft (200 m) exploits the fluid transparency of glass. Inside, the museum space is arranged on five levels accessible by a long and sinuous spiral staircase, which culminates in a huge terrace with extraordinary views of the Eiffel Tower and the city.

124-125 and 124 bottom
The museum's interiors feature a curious and fascinating series of large and well-lit spaces, associated with functional and connecting areas, interspersed with smaller and more shadowy zones that introduce visitors to the exhibitions. The bottom right photograph shows the evocative view that unfolds to visitors between the display area and the garden, looking towards the lush, decorative greenery.

125 Aboriginal paintings by eight famous Australian artists adorn the long, light-flooded corridors of the Research Center. The Eiffel Tower, just a few hundred feet away, can be seen in the photograph on the right. The site's proximity to such a powerful symbol of Paris and France was one of the greatest challenges faced by Nouvel. The new museum has attracted both praise and criticism, just like the Centre Pompidou, which is now an icon of the French capital.

Musée du Quai Branly

The collection cannot be pigeonholed into narrow categories, for it combines historical, artistic, anthropological and ethnographic elements. It totals over 300,000 artifacts – including 3500 on permanent display – which were formerly housed in the Musée de l'Homme and the Musée National des Arts d'Afrique et d'Océanie (which closed in 2003). The artifacts thus document the geographical areas of Africa, Asia, Oceania and the Americas, with special emphasis on pre-Columbian and Asian civilizations, the American Indians, Indonesia and Vietnam. Like the building carefully designed by Nouvel with the aim of achieving the perfect balance between container and contents, the exhibition layouts are presented to the visitor as paths of discovery through the various geographical areas and the cultures that have inhabited them. The exhibits are flanked by thematic displays with an educational purpose, which offer visitors the necessary information to understand the traditions and material cultures to which the artifacts belong. The building, its relationship with the surrounding greenery, its multifarious architecture and different colors are intended to symbolize the various cultures that, in the project created for the competition, the architect defined as "islands" that form a single "archipelago," which mingle in the interior while retaining their own distinctive features. The "box" rooms not only give the building its eccentric and modern external appearance, but also satisfy the display requirement of differentiating between areas that evoke highly diverse atmospheres.

In addition to the four main sections, dedicated to Oceania, Asia, America and Africa, the display also includes

four special exhibitions: the textile collection, comprising over 25,000 fabrics, dating mainly from the 19th and 20th centuries; the photography collection, with over 700,000 items from the mid 19th century to the present day; the musical instrument collection; and the history collection – the latter two inherited almost in their entirety from the Musée National des Arts d'Afrique et d'Océanie.

The museum is thus a showcase of distant lands and times, illustrating the civilizations of the past and also the work of contemporary artists. The aim is to create a path that distances itself from the traditional colonialist approach in favor of a more anthropological and less Westernized orientation, inspired by the work of Claude Lévi-Strauss, after whom the museum's theater is named.

EUROPE

126-127 and 127 The southern side of the 650-ft (200-m) museum building, exposed to the full light of the sun, is entirely glazed, while the northern side is home to the themed "boxes" dedicated to individual traditions and cultures. The complex has been designed to ensure a seamless visiting itinerary (or path of discovery). While it offers a surprising combination of different styles and materials, it nonetheless generates an impression of considerable unity, partly due to the great variety of objects that it houses. More than 3000 pieces are currently displayed, equivalent to just a hundredth part of the museum's possessions. An area of almost 55,000 sq. ft (5100 sq. m) is dedicated to the permanent exhibitions.

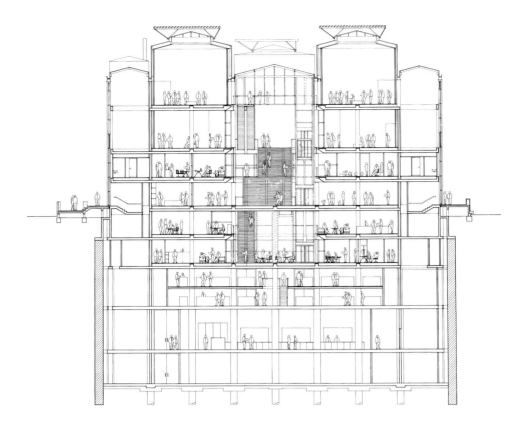

Musée Carré d'Art

NÎMES, FRANCE

The Carré d'Art gallery of contemporary art in Nîmes is one of the most successful examples of the use of contemporary design in a historic environment. It was opened to the public on May 8, 1993 and is situated in the heart of the ancient Provençal city, whose Roman origins are still very visible today.

The competition held for the design of the museum in 1984 was won by British architect Norman Foster, who rose to the challenge of creating a contemporary structure capable of blending and interacting with the historic urban setting, and even enhancing it – a feat that he repeated in London in 2000 with the British Museum's Great Court. In this case the environment was characterized by the ancient vestiges of the former Roman colony, for the gallery was built in the main square of the city, next to an Imperial Roman temple dedicated

to Gaius and Lucius Caesar, the grandsons of the emperor Augustus. During the 16th century the temple became popularly known as the Maison Carrée ("Square House"), and the gallery was named after it and contrasts with it, forming a harmonious confrontation between the architecture of the past and present.

Like the well-preserved ancient temple, the Carré d'Art has a very simple, regular rectangular structure. Its perimeter is entirely glazed, revealing its interior, and its central atrium evokes the typical structure of the traditional inner courtyards of the local houses. These features ensure that the entire building is bathed in natural light. The internal area of around 21,500 sq. ft (2000 sq. m) is distributed on 9 floors, 5 of which are sunk into the ground. The main display areas housing the permanent collection and temporary exhibitions are situated on the top two stories.

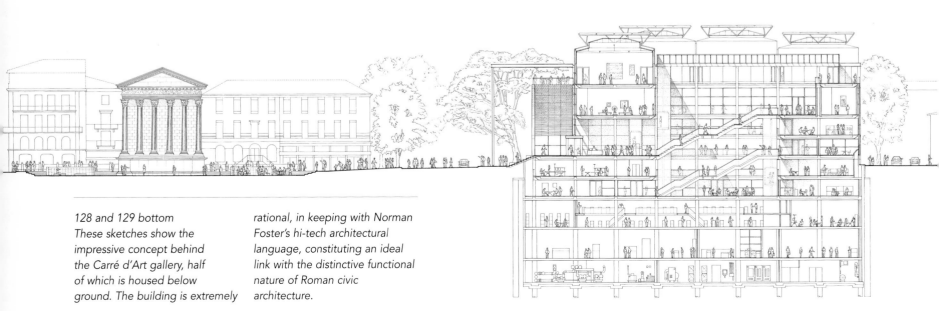

128 and 129 bottom These sketches show the impressive concept behind the Carré d'Art gallery, half of which is housed below ground. The building is extremely rational, in keeping with Norman Foster's hi-tech architectural language, constituting an ideal link with the distinctive functional nature of Roman civic architecture.

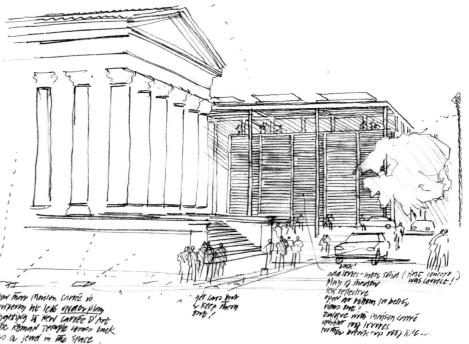

128-129 Expressly designed to contrast with and complement the Maison Carrée, its important neighbor, the Carré d'Art appears as a glass, concrete and steel structure on the western side of the city's historic center. Norman Foster's daring experiment has been a great success, for the museum and its library have revitalized the cultural life of Nîmes.

Musée Carré d'Art

The atrium, visible from outside, houses a large work by Richard Long entitled *Mud Line*, recording the movements of the artist and his handprints and welcoming visitors to the gallery. The Carré d'Art is home to a collection of contemporary art covering a period from the 1960s to the present day.

The collection was commenced in 1986 and currently features around 300 works, both donated and acquired by the National Contemporary Art Fund and the Regional Contemporary Art Fund of the Languedoc-Roussillon region. These works document and illustrate various artistic movements that have contributed to the development of 21st-century art, with particular emphasis on France and Europe. The French pieces include the production of important movements such as Nouveau Réalisme, Supports-Surfaces, BMTP and Figuration Libre, along with interesting works by famous contemporary artists including Arman, Martial Raysse,

Claude Viallat, Christian Boltanski and Bertrand Lavier. The French works are flanked by important pieces by Spanish artists, such as Miquel Barceló, Juan Muñoz, Cristina Iglesias, and Italian artists belonging to the Arte Povera movement, including Mario Merz, Jannis Kounellis, Giuseppe Penone and Giovanni Anselmo, and the Transavanguardia, such as Enzo Cucchi and Nicola de Maria. The gallery also boasts works by German artists, including Gerhard Richter, Sigmar Polke and Wolfgang Laib; the British sculptor and printmaker Barry Flanagan; and the American artists Allan Kaprow, Dan Flavin, Joseph Kosuth and Julian Schnabel.

The Carré d'Art also has several areas dedicated to cultural activities: a media library, a traditional library – unusually housed beneath ground level, but well-lit from the floor above – and a reading room, which is visible from the outside, while the terrace café offers visitors a splendid view over the city.

132 Urbain Vitry drew much of his inspiration for the complex designed to house the local abattoirs from the church of Saint-Sernin in Toulouse.

133 top The buildings that housed the slaughterhouses were renovated between 1997 and 2000 and converted into a gallery of modern and contemporary art.

133 center and bottom The buildings that now house the galleries, offices and public areas of the Les Abattoirs museum complex were designed in 1828 by French architect Urbain Vitry. The original design featured a semicircular arrangement of storerooms, two symmetrical rectangular blocks and a larger central building.

Musée Les Abattoirs

TOULOUSE, FRANCE

The Les Abattoirs gallery of modern and contemporary art is an interesting example of an older industrial complex that has been successfully converted to display and promote contemporary art. The buildings are situated close to the Garonne River in Toulouse, the capital of the fascinating French region of Midi-Pyrénées, also known as the "Pink City" due to the characteristic color of the local clay bricks of many of its buildings.

The Les Abattoirs museum complex houses the collections "inherited" from institutions such as the former Municipal Museum of Modern Art, the FRAC (Regional Contemporary Art Fund) and the Modern and Contemporary Art Gallery of Toulouse and Midi-Pyrénées, and is housed in a collection of buildings of particular historical and architectural interest. The structures in which the exhibitions, library, media library and cultural activities are housed were renovated and converted during the late 1990s, but the original industrial complex was designed by the 19th-century French architect Urbain Vitry. Vitry was responsible for a series of important buildings in Toulouse, including the Stock Exchange and the Commercial Court, and in 1828 he was commissioned to design a single complex to house all the abattoirs of the area. His project combined the simplicity, symmetry and rationalism of Neo-Classical architecture, interpreted with a modern twist, with the specific requirements of the immediate environment. Work commenced in 1828 and was completed in 1831, when the slaughterhouse was opened. Several structural changes were made the following year, and the complex was expanded between 1881 and 1891 by Achille Gaubert, and again in 1929 by Jean Montariol.

134-135 and 134 bottom
The collection of the Les
Abattoirs gallery comprises
around 2000 works, consisting of
paintings, sculptures, drawings,
installations and photographs
from the second half of the 20th
century, documenting the main
artistic movements (particularly
French) of the period. Much of
the collection was inherited from
the former Municipal Museum of
Modern Art, the FRAC (Regional
Contemporary Art Fund) and the
Modern and Contemporary Art
Gallery of Toulouse and Midi-
Pyrénées

135 top The central block of the
complex houses the gallery's
permanent collection. This cross-
section of the building shows the
arrangement of the display areas,
in which the itinerary leads from
the foyer on the ground floor to
the basement and the first floor.
Despite the restoration work, the
rooms have maintained their
original layout.

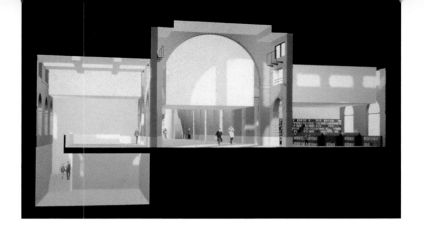

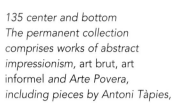

*135 center and bottom
The permanent collection
comprises works of abstract
impressionism, art brut, art
informel and Arte Povera,
including pieces by Antoni Tàpies,*
*Alberto Burri, Lucio Fontana,
Mario Merz, Robert Morris,
Robert Rauschenberg, Jean
Dubuffet, Marcel Duchamp and
Pierre Soulages. One of the
highlights of the gallery is the*
*room dedicated to Picasso, which
houses the striking La Dépouille
du Minotaure en Costume
d'Arlequin, the monumental stage
curtain that the artist created in
1936 for Romain Rolland's play.*

Musée Les Abattoirs

During the 19th century the abattoir complex had a large central structure with a basilica plan, clearly influenced by the marvelous church of Saint-Sernin in Toulouse in both its layout and its large window, which resembles the characteristic openings of Roman baths. Two symmetrical blocks were built either side, while a semicircular arrangement of structures was erected at the back, on the side overlooking the Garonne, to enclose the entire complex

The abattoirs closed down in 1989 and shortly after, in 1990, were officially included among the city's listed buildings. The 1990s witnessed the recovery of this unusual and fascinating complex as the result of a project jointly conducted by the French State, the city of Toulouse and the region of Midi-Pyrénées and aimed at identifying areas to dedicate to the display and study of contemporary art. Indeed, Vitry's industrial buildings were indicated as a possible solution in 1992, and in 1995 an architectural competition was held for the restoration and conversion of the slaughterhouse into a museum. The work, carried out between 1997 and 2000, took the form of an industrial archaeology and restoration project aimed at enhancing the existing buildings and converting them without making any invasive changes. The three-story central building is now home to the gallery's permanent collection, temporary exhibitions, an auditorium and a bookstore, while the side-blocks house offices and a media library. The former storerooms, arranged in a semicircle, have been transformed into a café and a sculpture workshop, while the smaller building in front of the entrance houses the rooms used for educational activities.

The permanent collection, whose layout further contributes to the successful merging of past and present, features around 2000 works of sculpture, painting, graphic art and photography by contemporary French and international artists, representing some of the most important artistic movements of the 20th century, such as abstract expressionism, *art brut* and Arte Povera. Featured artists include Antoni Tàpies, Alberto Burri, Lucio Fontana, Mario Merz, Robert Morris, Robert Rauschenberg, Jean Dubuffet, Marcel Duchamp and Pierre Soulages. One of the highlights of the gallery is the room dedicated to Picasso, which houses the striking *La Dépouille du Minotaure en Costume d'Arlequin*, the monumental stage curtain that the artist created in 1936 for Romain Rolland's play *Le Quatorze-Juillet*, presented at the Théâtre du Peuple in Paris to celebrate July 14th.

Oceanographic Museum
MONTE-CARLO, PRINCIPALITY OF MONACO

The Oceanographic Museum of Monaco is one of the world's leading specialist museums. It occupies a highly evocative site, perched on a cliff, and the stone building dominates the splendid view of the Principality. Its huge monumental façade is 280 ft (85 m) long and fairly eclectic in style, in keeping with contemporary Art Nouveau trends. It was the first museum of its kind and inspired all the other oceanographic museums in the world. It took over ten years to build the museum, which was commissioned by its founder, Prince Albert I of Monaco, who inaugurated it in 1910. The prince was not only the museum's patron, but also promoted important oceanographic research, establishing contact between scientists worldwide and promoting pioneering studies in the field.

Consequently, the statue of Albert I that greets visitors at the entrance to the museum, celebrates both his role as its founder and his contribution to the history of oceanography. Indeed, the prince entered the Navy aged just 18 and was a life-long lover and scholar of the sea.

The institute is not just a museum: the parts open to the public and serving as an educational museum are housed on three floors, while the lower stories are occupied by a library and large, well-equipped laboratories used for scientific research.

Nonetheless, the educational intent of the structure was pursued from the very outset and furthered greatly by the most famous of its directors, Jacques-Yves Cousteau, who occupied the post from 1957 to 1988. The main characteristic of this incredible museum is its ability to offer visitors greater knowledge of the underwater world through a series of tanks with specially recreated microclimates that illustrate the peculiarities and distinctive features of the fauna and flora of the most diverse geographical areas.

The Aquarium is one of the most important parts of the museum and allows visitors to admire the characteristics of open sea, lagoon, Mediterranean and tropical marine habitats. These tanks contain a wide variety of species, including blacktip and whitetip sharks, enormous batfish, bottom-dwelling rays, blowfish and groupers.

136 top A room of the museum is obviously dedicated to the funder of the institution, Prince Albert I, and is devoted to commemorate his life as a renowned seafarer and scientist.

136 bottom The museum's first poster announced the opening of the Oceanographic Museum of Monaco in 1910, thanks to its patron and founder, Prince Albert I of Monaco.

136-137 The Oceanographic Museum of Monaco is entirely built of stone and occupies a commanding site on a cliff between the headlands of Cap Martin and Cap Ail on the

Côte d'Azur. The building was designed by architect Paul Delefortrie and its construction required 11 years and over 100,000 tons of La Turbie stone.

138 The Whale Hall takes
its name from one of the
museum's most interesting
exhibits: a 65-ft (20-m) skeleton
of a whale.

139 top The Oceanographic
Museum was not founded
merely as a display area, but
also as a marine research center.

139 bottom left This photograph
shows the whaling ship used by
Prince Albert I during his marine
explorations.

139 bottom right The Conference
Room is decorated with a coffered
ceiling by the painter and architect
Emmanuel Cavaillé-Coll and with
paintings by Félix Hippolyte-Lucas.

Oceanographic Museum

One of the aquariums recreates the lagoon life of the coral reef, where clown fish, colorful unicorn fish and boxfish populate the upper zone, near the surface, and angelfish, electric rays and red groupers inhabit the depths.

The Tropical Room is home to a tank containing clown fish and anemones, along with many other weird and wonderful species, including the giant moray eel, cleaner shrimps, stonefish, toadfish, Cassiopea jellyfish, seahorses, razorfish and pineapple fish. Of course, there are also tanks housing more dangerous fish, such as lionfish, zebra moray eels and surgeonfish. In addition to the aquariums, the Caribbean section also displays a mechanical model illustrating the daily life of the nautilus. The Mediterranean section, on the other hand, is home to spiny lobsters, Norway lobsters, cuttlefish, sea bream, sea bass, gurnard and flying gurnard.

The large Conference Hall screens documentaries on the sea and its inhabitants, while the section dedicated to zoological oceanography houses an extensive collection of skeletons of all sizes, including that of a 65-ft (20-m) fin whale, swordfish, sawfish, giant Japanese spider crabs, a killer whale and a narwhal with a long ivory tusk, along with a series of display cases containing stuffed animals, including seals and penguins.

The museum also houses four of the large ships that were used for scientific expeditions conducted all over the world between 1884 and 1914, bearing witness to the research commenced by Prince Albert I. The rooms dedicated to physical oceanography often host temporary exhibitions that promote ongoing educational and teaching activities, while the applied oceanography room displays exhibits and reconstructions that recount humankind's close relationship and fascination with the sea through history, with tales of study, navigation and domination.

140-141 The microclimates associated to various kinds of marine waters and their ecosystems have been recreated in the tanks of the aquarium housed on the museum's lower floor.

141 top A statue commemorates Prince Albert I, who dedicated much of his life to the study of the sea. Models and instruments relating to his adventures are displayed in a room with a mosaic floor depicting marine motifs.

141 center The heart of the aquarium consists of the rooms dedicated to the Mediterranean and tropical seas, whose tanks containing dangerous fish are one of the museum's main attractions.

141 bottom The Oceanographic Museum is a tribute to both science and adventure. Indeed, the aquariums are flanked by several displays focusing on explorations, in this case of the Arctic.

Oceanographic Museum

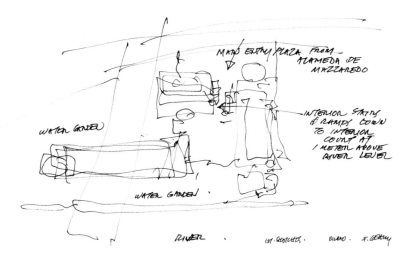

Guggenheim Museum
BILBAO, SPAIN

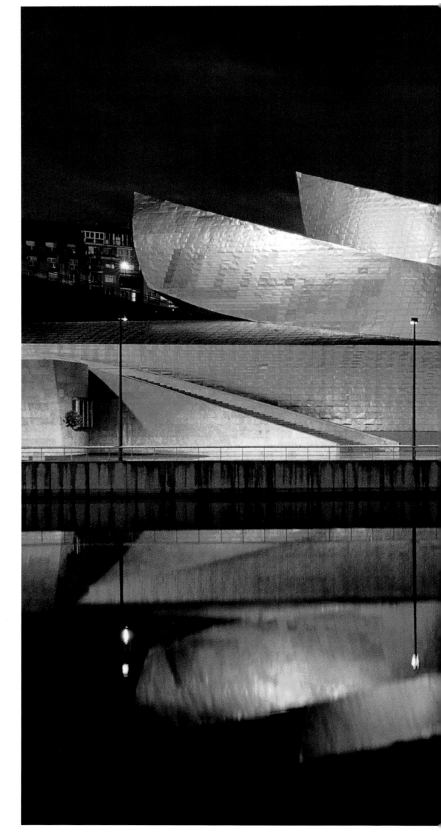

The Guggenheim Museum Bilbao has become an icon of the new style of museum architecture and design. It is undoubtedly one of the most famous examples of the policy to allow for the proper display of contemporary art, which requires bigger buildings and areas in order to house large installations and works. Indeed, a shift has occurred from the so-called "white cube" – a neutral building whose sole function is that of container and display case – to the more spectacular and evocative architectural expression of the museum itself as a work of art.

The Guggenheim Bilbao museum's symbolic value is, of course, associated with the international fame of the Guggenheim Foundation, of which it is part. Commencing with the headquarters (the Solomon R. Guggenheim Museum of New York) and under the innovative leadership of its director Thomas Krens, the Guggenheim Foundation has become synonymous with the popularization and diffusion of contemporary art worldwide, in step with the phenomenon of globalization.

The museum, opened in 1997, is part of a project (within a larger urban renewal plan) devised to revive an abandoned industrial area. The larger plan had been begun in 1998, and its aim was to inject new life into the city of Bilbao and the Basque Country in general.

142 These preliminary sketches for the design of the museum already reveal the general layout; top, the early plan shows the position of the museum in its urban setting in relation to the Nervión River and the La Salve bridge; bottom, Gehry's early elevation highlights the irregular volumes and forms of the future museum viewed from the north.

142-143 At night the museum is even more spectacular and striking, for a dramatic lighting system creates evocative plays of light on the titanium-clad walls.

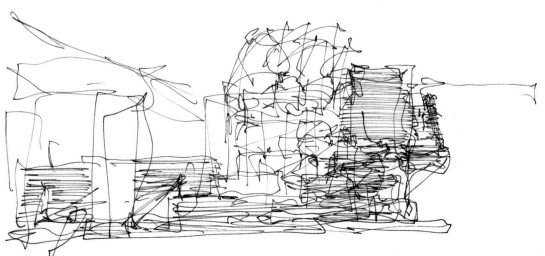

143 bottom In this preliminary sketch the architect has used irregular and sinuous lines to map out his initial idea of the building, which was subsequently refined by the use of highly sophisticated design software.

144 and 145 center The sinuous interweaving of the titanium walls and the different volumes emphasize the dynamic sculptural power of the building, which appears completely different during the day than at night.

145 top The main entrance is housed in an passageway in which the visitor comes face to face with the monumentality of the architecture. The apparent fluidity of the walls, heightened by the irregularity of the

volumes, enhances the characteristic sculptural nature of Gehry's designs, creating the sensation of a moving building.

145 bottom The titanium-clad walls alternate with windows

that allow natural light to filter into the display areas, while the structural parts are characterized by curved forms, creating a contemporary version of a Baroque-style virtuoso display.

Guggenheim Museum

146 *The huge atrium is one of the lightest areas of the interior of the Guggenheim Museum Bilbao: the natural light enters from overhead through a large glass skylight in the highest part of the building.*

147 *Visitors to the museum are greeted by an enormous atrium that allows access to the various floors and galleries. Inside the atrium the imposing dimensions of the building create a sensational perception of space, heightened by the convergence of curved lines and walls.*

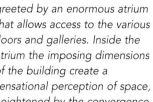

Guggenheim Museum

The city's objectives of distinctive urban reconstruction successfully merged with the Guggenheim Museum's wish to reinforce its own economic and cultural policies with another important presence in Europe.

Frank O. Gehry won the competition for the design of the museum, beating other famous names of the world of architecture, such as Arata Isozaky and Coop Himmelblau. Gehry designed the building with the use of the highly advanced CATIA software application, developed by the aeronautical industry and also used for the design of several French military aircraft. This particular program enabled him to create a building with numerous curved and irregular surfaces that help to transform it into a sort of contemporary cathedral with incredible sculptural power. The building is clad with around 30,000 sheets, made from 60 tons of titanium that was mined in Australia, refined in France, milled in Pittsburg and processed in Great Britain and Italy to a thickness of just 0.012 inches (0.3 mm). The sheets are positioned so that they change form, moving slowly with the pressure of the wind. The position of the museum heightens its impact yet further: it is situated on the banks of the River Nervión and an artificial lake, and the plays of light on the water are reflected in the shiny titanium panels that clad the building.

Guggenheim Museum

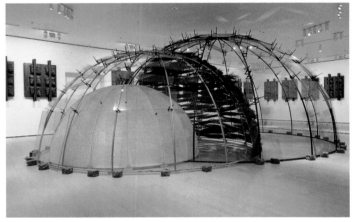

The effect from the outside is that of a material with an almost fluid, liquid, appearance that not only moves, but also changes color and tone according to the weather and the sunlight at different times of day. The inner structure of the building, divided up into three levels of exhibition galleries and a fourth story for the air-conditioning system, comprises a huge atrium about 165 ft (50 m) high, naturally lit by large windows overlooking the river. The wings are arranged around this atrium and house 19 galleries of different forms that are connected to it by a series of suspended curvilinear walkways, glass elevators and stair towers. The huge lowered vault has irregular openings through which overhead light enters.

The works displayed in the museum include a permanent collection partially dedicated to contemporary Spanish and Basque architects and a large collection focusing on important 20th- and 21st-century works and artists. These are supplemented with works from the other museums of the Guggenheim Foundation, depending on the calendar of temporary exhibitions. The many exhibits include works by leading contemporary artists, such as Richard Serra, Mark Rothko, Robert Rauschenberg, Jean-Michel Basquiat and Christian Boltanski. In front of the entrance stands Jeff Koons' enormous *Puppy* statue, completely covered with seasonal flowers, and permanent installations by Jenny Holzer, Louise Bourgeois, Yves Klein and Fujiko Nakaya.

The Guggenheim Museum Bilbao has both attracted great praise and fierce controversy because of its nature as a work of art; some argue that this competes with its primary role of exhibiting and enhancing works of art. However, it remains an unrivaled example of complex and efficient design and an icon of not only a new way of proposing and devising space destined for art, but also of the history of contemporary architecture.

148 top Three Red Spanish Venuses by Jim Dine (1997) is the work of one of the leading figures of the American Pop art movement, whose main characteristic was originally the investigation of popular and commercial culture.

148 top center Wall Drawing #831 by Sol LeWitt (1997) features colored geometric combinations that delimit irregular shapes, capable of altering the relationship between the visitor and the room.

148 bottom center Unreal City by Mario Merz (1985) is one of the artist's famous igloos. The subject is one of the artist's favorites, which he uses to reflect on the relationship between man, art and society.

148 bottom and 149 A large area of the museum is dedicated to installations, such as the monumental Snake by Richard Serra (left) and Labyrinth by Robert Morris (1974, left), which invite the visitor to interact with them.

150-151 and 150 bottom
The majestic façade of the Prado
Museum in Madrid, designed by
architect Juan de Villanueva, is
Neoclassical in style, with a Doric
portico flanked by two large
colonnaded Ionic wings. A statue
of Diego Velázquez, one of the
greatest Spanish painters, stands
in front of the museum entrance.

151 top Young visitors in front of
Francisco Goya's Blindman's Buff
and The Stilt-Walkers, as they
learn about one of the greatest
Spanish masters.

151 bottom Architect Juan
de Villaneuva's admiration of
Palladio's work is apparent in
many parts of the Prado, such
as this Neoclassical dome.

Prado Museum
MADRID, SPAIN

The history of the Prado Museum commenced in 1775, when King Charles III of Spain (1759-1778), commissioned the architect Juan de Villaneuva to design a natural-science museum, located in the "meadow" (*prado*) where the citizens of Madrid enjoyed strolling, in the area adjoining the Buen Retiro palace. Villaneuva used local stone from the Sierra de Guadamarra, such as the granite of the doorways, window surrounds and columns, and white Colmenar limestone for the bases. The architect adorned the Neo-Classical building with features borrowed from the Palladian villas that he had much admired during his travels in Italy. A botanical garden, an observatory and a chemistry laboratory were also planned in the museum grounds. However, construction was not completed until the reign of Ferdinand VII (1813-1833). During the bloody Peninsular War, Napoleon's troops used the building as a barracks, and subsequently local residents used it as a stone quarry when attempting to rebuild houses destroyed in the conflict.

The idea of creating a museum to rival the Louvre was proposed following the death of Charles III, during the period in which his successor, Charles IV (1778-1804), was dealing with the political repercussions of the French Revolution. The museum was initially housed in the Buenavista Palace, and named the Josephine Museum, after Joseph I Bonaparte, who had briefly attempted to rule the nation. In 1814, following the petitions of the Academy of Fine Arts and the interest in the project shown by his wife, Queen Maria Isabel, Ferdinand VII transformed Villanueva's building into the Royal Museum of Painting and Sculpture, displaying collections put together over the centuries by the Spanish rulers. The renovation and interior decoration of the building was completed about 15 years later. The museum opened on November 19, 1819, but sadly Queen Maria Isabel – often considered the true founder of the Prado – died before she had the chance to see her dream come true. In 1868 the museum was nationalized and assumed the name of Museo del Prado, marking the transition from royal collection to national museum.

The Prado's collections acquired from the old Trinidad Museum and those taken from the Escorial Palace and from Madrid's churches and museums following the Spanish Civil War (1936-1939) remain an important element of the museum's holdings. Another significant element is the earlier royal collections the Prado now houses. These document the aesthetic tastes and love of art of a long series of Spanish sovereigns across the dynasties, from the House of Castile to those of Habsburg and Bourbon. Indeed, the Spanish rulers were particularly attentive to cultural production and were great patrons of internationally renowned artists. A powerful example is the close relationship between Charles V (1516-1555) and Titian, from whom Philip II (1556-1598) also purchased great works, such as the artist's *Self-Portrait* and *Venus and Adonis*, along with the *Garden of Earthly Delights* by

Hieronymus Bosch and *The Descent from the Cross* by Rogier van der Weyden. Philip IV (1621-1665) enriched the collection with 32 masterpieces by Rubens, purchased following the artist's death, as well as precious works by Mantegna, Raphael, Dürer, Titian, Veronese and Tintoretto. The king also appointed Diego Velázquez, the leading Spanish artist of his day, as court painter. The Prado boasts numerous masterpieces by the great artist, including the famous *Las Meninas* ("The Maids of Honor").

Philip IV's successor, Charles II (1661-1700), managed to save the royal gallery from the covetous grasp of his avid wife by means of a legal proviso that he subsequently extended to all the royal collections, which Philip V (1700-1746) expanded with works by

152-153 The arrangement of the works in the Prado Museum is generally fairly conservative, following the traditional art gallery layout. The photograph shows one of the ground floor corridors housing the extensive collection of Italian painting, which dates from the 14th to the 19th century.

152 bottom An extraordinary array of Spanish paintings, dating from the 12th to the 19th century, is housed in various rooms on each of the three display floors. The photograph shows the long first-floor corridor hung with works by artists such as Ribera, Ribalta and Murrillo.

Prado Museum

153 top During the 19th and 20th centuries the museum was subject to extensive program of renovation and enlargement. The old vault of the long, wide central gallery was removed and rebuilt in concrete in 1927, while a new staircase leading up to the first floor was built in 1945.

153 bottom The museum's rich collection of sculpture includes statues, busts, reliefs, vases, columns and fragments of Greek and Roman statuary. The antiquities collection was purchased by Philip V during the 18th century and displayed in the Palace of the Granja, before being transferred to the Prado.

Titian, Raphael, Poussin, and Orazio and Artemisia Gentileschi. Charles IV (1788-1808) is closely bound up with Francisco Goya, who painted hundreds of masterpieces now housed in the Prado, including *The Third of May 1808*, the *Clothed Maja* and *Naked Maja* portraits, and the series of cartoons for the tapestries produced by the Royal Factory of Santa Barbara. The works by Doménikos Theotokópoulos, known as El Greco, on the other hand, were not commissioned by royalty and are mainly more recent acquisitions from suppressed religious institutions. They occupy an entire room of the museum. In addition to rooms dedicated to Velázquez, Goya, El Greco, Titian and Raphael, the Prado also features sections devoted to classical sculpture and to German, Flemish, Dutch, French, Italian and – of course – Spanish art, spanning a period from the 14th to the 18th century.

Museo Nacional Centro de Arte Reina Sofía

MADRID, SPAIN

The Reina Sofía Museum, like the Prado, can claim to be one of most prestigious museums in Madrid and indeed in Spain. On September 1, 1992 King Juan Carlos and Queen Sofia of Spain inaugurated the permanent collection of the Museo Nacional Centro de Arte Reina Sofía, making what had initially been established as a venue for temporary exhibitions into a true museum. The Reina Sofía is situated in the city center, near the Plaza de Cibeles, in a building designed in the late 18th century by the architect Francesco Sabatini as the San Carlos hospital. In 1977 a royal decree declared the structure a national historical and artistic monument, thwarting the intentions of those who had suggested its demolition. During the 1980s restoration commenced under Antonio Fernández Alba and was completed by José Luis Iñíguez de Onzoño and Antonio Vázquez de Castro, with the collaboration of British architect Ian Ritchie, who designed the spectacular glass and steel towers that house the elevators serving the various floors of the museum.

In 1986 several areas of the building, then known as the Centro de Arte Reina Sofía, were opened. They were initially used only to host temporary shows under the direction of Carmen Giménez, head of the Ministry of Culture's National Exhibition Center. The turning point came in 1988, when the Center acquired a more prestigious and important role with the royal decree that turned it into a National Museum to replace the former Museo Español de Arte Contemporáneo (MEAC). The institution's first director was Tomás Llorens, who held the position until 1990. His successor was María del Corral, who directed the museum until 1994, when José Guirao Cabrera was appointed. The 1988 royal decree also established that the museum's collections would be formed by those of the former MEAC, expanded by a policy of acquisitions and all the 20th-century works of the Prado Museum, including Picasso's famous *Guernica* (1937), which is still one of the Reina Sofía's best-known and most emblematic works. Other important pieces were acquired through private donations, sometimes by the artists themselves, as in the case of Salvador Dalí. However, many of the works by Spanish artists, including the extraordinary ones by Joan Miró, were purchased under the provisions of the legislative decree passed in 1985 to enhance and increase the national artistic heritage.

The current layout of the museum is even more arresting and modern.

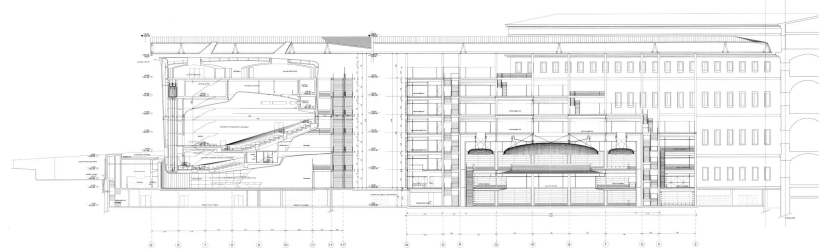

154 top Saved from demolition by its architectural merit, the Reina Sofía is now a contemporary setting for masterpieces such as Picasso's Guernica, formerly housed in the Prado.

154 bottom The Spanish national flag flies alongside one of the two 115-foot-tall elevator towers, which have been added to the 18th-century building.

154-155 and 155 bottom Transparent, minimalist additions have redesigned the façade of the former hospital, whose renovation and expansion project (bottom) was also aimed at redeveloping the square in front of the museum and the Atocha district. The new structure was designed to allow more direct contact between the public and architecture and the environment.

Museo Nacional Centro de Arte Reina Sofía

It was designed by the famous French architect Jean Nouvel, who won the competition held in 1999 to select a project for the expansion of the museum, which required more exhibition space. Nouvel created a large and striking extension, which was formally opened in October 2005. The construction of the new triangular wing took four years, and the resulting structure is composed of three buildings connected to each other and to the original museum building, with a covered courtyard in the space between them. These striking large new areas house an auditorium, library and additional exhibition space, more than doubling the area of the old museum. The impact of the new structures is heightened by the use of innovative materials, such as the bright red fiberglass and polyester cladding of the auditorium.

The Reina Sofía is home to one of Europe's most outstanding collections of 20th-century art, which not only comprise Picasso's already mentioned masterpiece commemorating the destruction of Guernica in 1937, and works by Dalí and Miró, but also pieces by other leading Spanish artists, such as José Gutiérrez Solana, Pablo Gargallo and Julio González. Furthermore, the museum also houses works by international artists including Sonia and Robert Delaunay, Jacques Lipchitz, Juan Gris, Alexander Calder, examples of American minimalism by Ellsworth Kelly and Donald Judd, and the conceptual art of Bruce Nauman. The spacious new wing by Jean Nouvel is able to host temporary exhibitions and expands the role of the gallery with activities aimed at promoting, studying and enhancing contemporary artistic production.

156-157 and 156 bottom left
A modern covered agora is the focal point of the museum extension designed by Jean Nouvel and opened in 2005. Three new buildings and the rear façade of Sabatini's building are arranged around a large cultural courtyard. When viewed from the outside (bottom left), the huge roof can be seen to overlap the perimeter of the inner square.

156 bottom right and 157 top
Bright red is the dominant color of Nouvel's extension. The parts added with the French architect's project include a café and a restaurant (bottom right), with a spectacular roof, and two auditoriums (top) able to seat 450 and 200 people. The new extension has made the Reina Sofía one of the largest and best-structured museums of contemporary art in the world.

158-159 Calatrava's buildings in the City of Arts and Sciences undoubtedly constitute one of the most impressive cultural complexes in the history of architecture. The architect's "organic" structures are multiplied by reflections and perspective effects, creating the illusion of living and perpetually changing architecture, and this impression is reinforced by the mobile nature of some of the structural components.

158 bottom The long "spine" of the Museu de les Ciències reaches towards the hemispherical Palau de les Arts opera house, visible on the right of the photograph.

159 Top, situated beyond the Hemisfèric (the first part of the "City" to be completed in 1989), the science museum was inaugurated in 2000. Bottom, the Umbracle is a two-story car park and walkway, which constitutes Calatrava's most recent contribution to the City of Arts and Sciences (2001).

City of Arts and Sciences

VALENCIA, SPAIN

The Ciutat de les Arts i les Ciències (City of Arts and Sciences) is an extraordinary, innovative and cutting-edge architectural complex that houses five different buildings dedicated to three main themes: the Arts, Sciences and Nature. It is housed in the dry riverbed that was once occupied by the Turia, on a site of approximately 3.75 million sq. ft (350,000 sq. m). The plans drawn up for this multipurpose center were part of a larger scheme to revive the entire city of Valencia, and this extraordinary green area in particular, and relaunch it as a tourist destination. The project for the redevelopment and transformation of the Turia area into a park was designed and built between 1981 and 1988 by architect Ricardo Bofill, who recovered a strip around 5 miles (8 km) long, stretching from east to west of Valencia, and covered it with cycle paths, parks and

sports facilities. The result was a dynamic new center, which was immediately and enthusiastically adopted by the local people.

The area is now home to the museum complex designed by Valencian architect Santiago Calatrava and commenced in 1996. Calatrava's buildings are a fine example of contemporary architecture that respects both the environment and the Mediterranean spirit of the city, particularly in the use of light and the plays of color between the dazzling white of the concrete and the blue of the sky and the pools of water. The buildings are very different from each other, but at the same time harmonious. The Palau de les Arts Reina Sofía, inaugurated in 2005, is a monumental building over 245 ft (75 m) high and covering an area of almost 450,000 sq. ft (41,800 sq. m), which is dedicated to the creation, promotion and diffusion of all the performing arts.

City of Arts and Sciences

160 *The Museu de les Ciències Príncipe Felipe is the largest structure of the complex, covering an area of over 250,000 square feet on three levels. Calatrava's innovative style is best* *expressed in public spaces: his light, bright creations emphasize the visual aspect of architecture and their skillful engineering makes them immediately recognizable.* 161 *The inspiration of nature is very evident in the science museum, where the old-fashioned notion of "do not touch" has been replaced by fully interactive displays.*

It offers three auditoriums – including an open-air one – housed within two symmetrical concrete shells. The building is connected to the others by a panoramic walkway, also designed by Calatrava.

The Hemisfèric, opened in 1998, takes the striking form of a giant human eye, which is partly completed by its reflection in the pool beneath it. It covers an area of over 250,000 sq. ft (23,225 sq. m) and is home to the planetarium. The Umbracle was inaugurated in 2001. It houses an indoor car park and its second and highest story allows visitors to enjoy extraordinary views along the panoramic "Stroll of the Sculptures," from which the other buildings can be seen. The Oceanogràfic, opened in 2003, was designed by architect Felix Candela and is one of the largest aquariums in Europe. It covers an outdoor

area of 1.2 million sq. ft (112,000 sq. m), while its interior allows visitors to enjoy spectacular itineraries among the tanks and their many inhabitants (over 40,000 specimens).

However, perhaps the most striking building of the architectural complex is Calatrava's huge and fascinating work that recalls the abandoned skeleton of a dinosaur, embodying the Spanish architect's desire to create buildings similar in shape to various life forms. It is known as the Museu de les Ciències Príncipe Felipe and was opened in 2000. It is a very large museum with three stories, each covering an area of about 85,000 sq. ft (7900 sq. m). The long building has a rectangular plan, allowing it to contain a huge exhibition hall. The internal concrete structure is visible in five monumental tree-like pillars, which house the stairs and elevators that allow access to the upper stories.

City of Arts and Sciences

162 A view of the interior of the science museum reveals the importance that Calatrava assigned to the structural skeleton of the building, which forms virtually all the visible part of the work.

163 top One of the distinctive features of Calatrava's works is their easy access – as shown by this escalator – which is not always immediately evident due to the complexity of their design.

163 bottom These sinewy ribs clearly reveal the architect's interest in natural sciences and anatomy, and the structure possesses the perfect efficiency of a limb or an organ.

One of the building's main characteristics is the play of reflected light that forms between the large windows and the water of the surrounding pool. These shimmering effects create the impression of architecture that is both fragile and monumental, like the "skeletal" structure of the museum, similar to a gutted building, filled only with reflections, water and evanescent light. Inside, the museum houses educational displays on themes ranging from the purely scientific, concerning the research fields of biology and physics, to the sphere of the history of technology and communications. The displays make extensive use of interactive multimedia technology, due to a specific policy aimed at involving and teaching visitors as much as possible.

Valencia's Ciutat de les Arts i les Ciències is an exceptionally interesting complex, both from an architectural standpoint and as an active cultural and museum center. After dark all the buildings are illuminated, creating an even more extraordinary spectacle.

164-165 Viewed from the Umbracle, through an impressing scenario of interlacing ribs, the Museu de les Ciències (with a Christmas tree in front of it) seems inextricable from the structure of the bridge itself, visually forming a new architectural element. The visitor is struck by the same sensation of multiplication of the real architectural structures in many other points of the City of Arts and Sciences.

165 The choice of forms took priority over engineering considerations in the design of the science museum: the three-dimensional structure was developed around the design itself, and the most advanced techniques of civil engineering were subsequently applied to the network of ribbing, whose ubiquity is never overpowering. The final touch is the architect's choice of pale colors, which lighten the structure, banishing any heaviness.

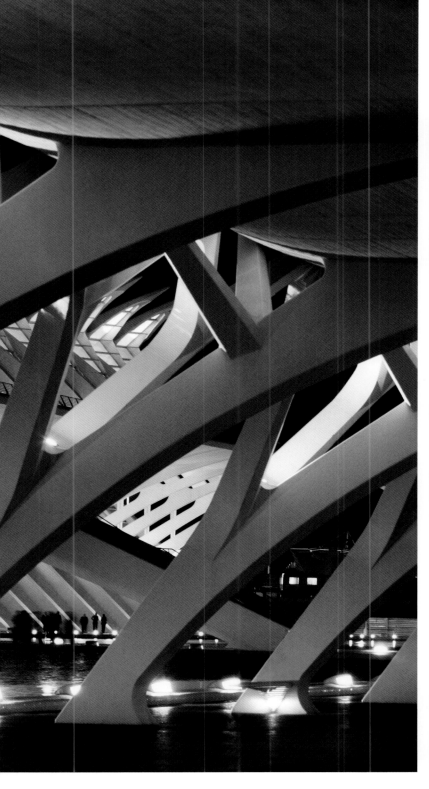

City of Arts and Sciences

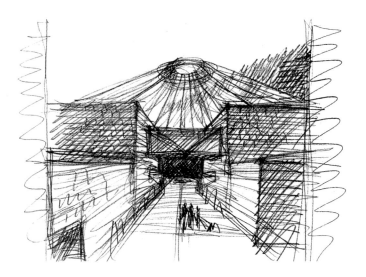

MART

ROVERETO, ITALY

ART – the acronym for Museum of Modern and Contemporary Art of Trento and Rovereto – is one of the most famous galleries of its kind in Italy. The museum was designed by the noted Swiss architect Mario Botta, with the collaboration Giulio Andreolli, an engineer from Rovereto, and was formally opened to the public in 2002. The building occupies a strategic site in Rovereto, between the hills and Corso Bettini, one of the main streets leading to the town's historic district. It is not immediately visible, except for a little driveway that reveals its position, set back from the street, and that leads to the entrance of the museum through a huge atrium topped by a spectacular cupola.

One of the difficulties the architect encountered was that of inserting such a large and intentionally modern building in a historic urban setting, close to important palaces, such as Palazzo Alberti and Palazzo dell'Annona, which offer unobstructed views of the surrounding hills and mountains. MART's particularly evocative interior space derives from the entrance piazza at the heart of the museum complex,

devised as a sort of contemporary agora with a diameter of 130 ft (40 m), capable of accommodating over 1200 people. It is topped by an 80-ft/24-m-high glass cupola with steel grilles and a central opening, which heightens its resemblance to a sort of updated Pantheon. A circular fountain stands in the center of this entrance area, often surrounded by installations or sculptures, such as the anthropomorphic creations of artist Mimmo Paladino,

166 top The new MART – Museum of Modern and Contemporary Art of Trento and Rovereto – complex was designed by Mario Botta and Giulio Andreolli, *and inaugurated in 2002. It also comprises a municipal library, an auditorium and a building for exhibitions and cultural events staged by the city council.* *166 center and bottom Botta's sketch and the cross-sections of the museum show how he has created the building through the composition of highly geometric* *volumes, arranged around the large, partially covered space of the entrance square, while a "suspended walkway" links the museum's two semicircular wings.*

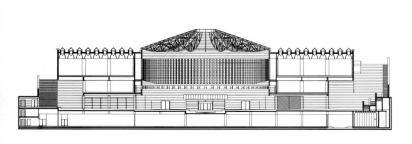

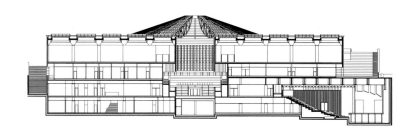

166-167 and 167 bottom
Following the opening of the museum, a series of sculptures by Mimmo Paladino, an artist associated with the Italian Transavanguardia movement, were temporarily arranged around the circular fountain in the center of the entrance piazza, greeting visitors and adorning the large covered area.

168-169 The galleries used to stage exhibitions are located on the third (and highest) floor of the museum.

168 bottom left The reception area is situated at the entrance to the museum.

168 bottom right The building is clad with yellow slabs of Vicenza stone, marked by vertical openings, which allow the natural lighting of the interior while enabling visitors to look out.

169 The atrium allows access to the staircase, with two symmetric flights of steps leading to the display rooms and to the basement, which houses the archive and the library.

MART

which were strikingly arranged here during the first few months after opening and subsequently transferred to the permanent collection. The entire building is clad with slabs of yellow Vicenza stone and is characterized by a semicircular shape rhythmically punctuated by vertical openings that allow the natural light from the cupola and large skylight to filter into the interior, creating theatrical lighting effects that vary according to the time of day. The interior is arranged on four spacious levels, two of which are dedicated to the permanent and temporary exhibitions and the other two to offices, teaching areas, the library and archives.

The museum's permanent collection consists of some 7000 works of art, comprising paintings, drawings and sculptures, which have gradually been pieced together through a significant series of acquisitions, but above all by gifts of private collections. The largest and most important part of this heritage consists of the core of Futurist works, particularly those by the Rovereto artist Fortunato Depero, of which the museum possesses some 3000 valuable pieces. Much of the 20th-century archive also concentrates on the Italian Futurist avant-garde art movement. The artifacts are housed in the basement of the museum. In addition to the Fortunato Depero archive there are also archives dedicated to other important artists, including Gino Severini, Carlo Carrà and Thayaht, around whom the Centro Internazionale del Futurismo developed.

The collection of 20th-century works allows visitors to trace the key stages in the development of both Italian 20th-century art and the production of internationally renowned contemporary artists. Italian 20th-century art is represented by works of artists such as Mario Sironi, Giorgio Morandi, Fausto Melotti, Giorgio De Chirico, Felice Casorati and Emilio Vedova. More recent acquisitions include works by American Pop artists from the New York collection of Ileana Sonnabend, featuring pieces by Andy Warhol, Robert Rauschenberg and Roy Lichtenstein; works by contemporary international artists such as Bruce Nauman and Richard Long; and works by Italian Arte Povera artists, including Giulio Paolini, Alighiero Boetti and Mario Merz. The museum also displays major pieces from the Panza di Biumo Collection, mainly by American artists of the 1980s and 1990s.

In addition to the main building, MART – Museum of Modern and Contemporary Art of Trento and Rovereto – is a museum complex with two other premises: the Renaissance Palazzo delle Albere in Trento and the museum house of Fortunato Depero in Rovereto.

MART

170 top Michelangelo Pistoletto is one of the most representative artists of the Arte Povera movement, founded in Italy during the 1960's. One of his works displayed at MART is Orchestra di Stracci,Quartetto (1968), shown in the photograph.

170 center and bottom MART's permanent collection offers an overview of some of the most important artistic movements of the 20th and 21st centuries. Italian art is represented largely by the extensive Futurist collection, but also by Arte Povera works.

170-171 The huge display areas are able to house large works and installations, such as the environmental installation by British artist Richard Long (b. 1945), one of the leading figures of the Land art movement, shown in the foreground of the photograph.

171 bottom The Panza di Biumo collection allows visitors to admire works by contemporary artists – mostly American and relatively unknown to the Italian public – including Peter Shelton, Roni Horn, Lawrence Carroll, David Simpson, Max Cole, Stuart Arends and Ford Beckman.

172 One of the Uffizi's most precious architectural gems is the gallery that runs along the entire top floor of Vasari's horseshoe-shaped building, around the Uffizi's inner square and along the bank of the river Arno.

173 The open loggia of Vasari's original design was subsequently adapted for Grand Duke Francesco I, who commissioned its conversion into a gallery to display the Medici family's collection of statuary, which was transferred there in 1581.

Uffizi Gallery

FLORENCE, ITALY

The Uffizi Gallery, which is closely bound up with the history of the Medici family and the cultural ferment that had always distinguished the Florentine court, is one of the most famous examples of a building designed expressly as a museum.

Cosimo I became Grand Duke of Tuscany in 1534, when aged just 18. He was responsible for a series of urban projects aimed at enhancing his city, concentrating in particular on Piazza della Signoria and the surrounding areas. As part of this scheme he decided to construct a building to house the government offices (*uffizi*) on the first floor and to house and display the Medici's important art collections on the second floor. The famous painter and architect Giorgio Vasari was engaged to design the palace, whose construction was commenced in 1560. The building, located south of Piazza della Signoria, and overlooking the River Arno on one side, was built entirely from gray stone, and the two wings of the horseshoe-shaped structure were connected by the existing buildings of the Zecca Vecchia and the Loggia dei Lanzi.

In 1565, on the occasion of the marriage of Cosimo's son Francesco to Joanna of Austria, Vasari designed a raised passageway between Palazzo Vecchio and Palazzo Pitti. In the space of just six months, the architect built what is now known as the Vasari Corridor. This extraordinary aerial passage enabled the Grand Dukes to move in safety between Palazzo Vecchio and Palazzo Pitti, via Ponte Vecchio and the Oltrarno district.

However, Vasari and his patron both died in 1574, and the building was completed by Buontalenti in 1580 for Francesco I. Buontalenti designed the Porta delle Suppliche, famous for its unusual "split tympanum" invention; the octagonal Tribuna, destined to house the treasures of the Medici collections; and

Uffizi Gallery

174-175 Francesco I decided to use the loggia on the top floor of the Uffizi as a gallery to house ancient statues and portraits of the Medici family and illustrious men. In 1579–81 the vaults of the gallery were frescoed with grotesque motifs inspired by ancient Roman murals, particularly those of Nero's Golden House.

174 bottom In 1996 the East Corridor was painstakingly restored, revealing the full splendor of the decorations and frescoed ceilings commissioned by Francesco I when he ordered its conversion into a gallery to house the antique sculptures and busts of illustrious members of the Medici family.

175 top left This staircase leads from the West Corridor to the Vasari Corridor, commissioned by Cosimo de' Medici and built in 1565 as a private passageway connecting Palazzo Pitti to Palazzo Vecchio and the Uffizi.

175 top right One of the most evocative views offered by the magnificent Uffizi Gallery is that of the loggia of the piano nobile, where the morning light is allowed to flood through great windows exposed to the east.

175 bottom The Niobe Room, built in 1779–80 by Gaspare Paoletti to house the statues from Villa Medici and the paintings by Rubens depicting the Triumphs of Henry IV of France, which were later moved to another room.

the Medici theater, which was subsequently partially converted into a gallery. In 1581 Francesco I decided to use the long loggia on the top floor of the Uffizi as a gallery to house the ancient statues and the portraits of the Medici family, and had the ceilings frescoed with grotesque motifs. Francesco's successor, his brother Ferdinando, was a learned man and added to the gallery with the "Gioviana" series of portraits of famous men and with the Geographical Maps and Mathematics rooms. Ferdinando also established the Manifatture delle Pietre Dure (precious stones workshop) in 1588 and commissioned the

new entrance, although it was not actually built until much later by Zanobi del Rosso.

The gallery remained unaltered for almost half a century, before gradually resuming its expansion, fueled by the acquisitions of Cosimo III (1670-1723), and subsequently by the gallery's most famous and important bequest, made by Cosimo's daughter Anna Maria Luisa in 1737. Indeed, this noblewoman left the city of Florence an extraordinary collection of works of art on the condition that nothing was ever removed from the city.

176-177 The grotesque motifs decorating the ceiling of the first corridor, packed with scholarly and mythological references, were begun by Antonio Tempesta and continued by Alessandro Allori, assisted by Ludovico Buti, Giovanmaria Butteri, Giovanni Bizzelli and Alessandro Pieroni. Ferdinando I added to the gallery commenced by his brother Francesco I with the "Gioviana" collection started by his father Cosimo I.

Uffizi Gallery

178 top The three large frescoes in the Map Room, painted by Lodovico Buti in 1589, depict maps drawn up by Stefano Buonsignori depicting the areas of Florence, Siena and Elba ruled by the Medici family.

178 bottom left The Miniatures Room was commissioned in the late 16th century. Its original plan resembled that of the Tribune, although its current form is the result of its renovation by Zanobi del Rosso.

178 bottom right and 179 The Tribuna has an octagonal plan and opens on to the East Corridor. It was built by Bernardo Buontalenti and features a decorative scheme based on the four elements.

Uffizi Gallery

Grand Duke Leopoldo I reorganized the Uffizi and opened the gallery to the public in 1769, after having entrusted the assistant antiquarian, Luigi Lanzi, with reordering the collections according to educational criteria aimed at aiding their enjoyment by visitors. In the mid-19th century it was decided to transform the Uffizi into a picture gallery, and consequently a series of works were moved from the Uffizi to the Archaeological Museum and the National Museum of the Bargello. During the same period Vasari's original project was completed with the creation of 28 marble statues of illustrious Tuscans, which were set in the niches on the outside of the building. The Uffizi was the target of a bomb attack in 1993, which damaged the Vasari Corridor and part of the gallery, and required the restoration of both the building and several pieces in the collection.

The works housed in the Uffizi span the period from antiquity to the first half of the 18th century. Highlights include emblematic Florentine early Renaissance works, including masterpieces by Masaccio, Fra Angelico, Paolo Uccello, Filippo Lippi and the Pollaiuolo brothers, and the world's most important collection of works by Sandro Botticelli, including his two most famous paintings: the Primavera (ca. 1482) and The Birth of Venus (ca. 1485). Other great masterpieces include The Adoration of the Magi by Gentile da Fabriano, the Doni Tondo by Michelangelo, The Battle of San Romano by Paolo Uccello, the Venus of Urbino by Titian, the Madonna of the Goldfinch and Self-Portrait by Raphael, the Madonna of the Long Neck by Parmigianino, and the Medusa by Caravaggio.

In addition, the gallery's collections contain numerous masterpieces by many other great masters including Leonardo, Perugino, Signorelli, Bellini, Giorgione, Mantegna, Pontormo and Bronzino to Dürer, Rubens and Rembrandt, as well as rooms dedicated to Flemish and German Renaissance works.

Vatican Museums

VATICAN CITY

The Vatican Museums, which include many large and small museums, are home to a huge historical and artistic legacy; all bear witness to the development of papal collecting and patronage from Renaissance onward.

The Vatican Museums' eventful history spans several centuries. It commenced with Julius II, who, following his election in 1503 and fired by a love of culture and the classical arts typical of the Renaissance spirit, gathered together and displayed a collection of sculpture in the "Courtyard of Statues." The antique statues of the *Apollo Belvedere*, the *Laocoön* group and the *Sleeping Ariadne* were thus installed in the courtyard of the Belvedere Palace, commissioned by Innocent VIII (1484-1492) and built to Pollaiuolo's design by Jacopo da Pietrasanta, and later extended by Bramante, who was engaged by Julius II himself (1503-1513).

The Vatican, which was gradually assuming international importance as a cultural center, already had a very substantial library: the Vatican Apostolic Library, which can still be visited today. It was commenced by Nicholas V (1447-1455) and completed by Sixtus IV (1471-1484), and houses a collection of over 60,000 extraordinarily valuable manuscripts.

The collections commenced by Julius II continued to be expanded by his successors, Leo X (1513-1521), Clement VII (1523-1534), Paul III (1534-1549), Pius IV (1559-1565) and Pius V (1566-1572). The transformation of the holdings into exhibits maintained in a museum occurred between the 18th and 19th centuries, when the cultural role of the Vatican became increasingly recognized, in part because of its extraordinary archaeological collections. Clement XI (1700-1721) commenced the acquisition of inscriptions, which was continued by Benedict XIV (1740-1758), who founded the Gallery of Inscriptions. Popes Clement XIV (1769-1774) and Pius VI (1775-1799) subsequently extended the gallery's collections, as did Pius VII (1800-1823), who in 1802 appointed Antonio Canova as its curator. Today the Gallery of Inscriptions forms part of the Chiaramonti Museum, which has more than 5000 pagan and Christian inscriptions, and the so-called New Wing that houses 2nd-century mosaics and a collection of antique statuary, including the *Augustus of Prima Porta*, *The Nile* and *The Resting Satyr* by Praxiteles.

Another important event in the history of the Vatican Museums was the foundation of the Pio-Clementino Museum, established by Clement XIV and enlarged by Pius VI, who were both fiercely determined to enrich the Vatican's collection of classical sculpture yet further. The museum was opened in 1771 and was incorporated in the extension of the Vatican Palace following 15 years of imposing construction work that involved the Belvedere Courtyard – known as the Cortile Ottagono – in

180 left The Vatican Museums are housed in an immense architectural complex, built on a site that was inhabited from the 5th century B.C. The buildings are arranged principally around the Pigna and Belvedere courtyards.

180 right The Cortile della Pigna takes its name from the Roman bronze pinecone that was found near the Baths of Agrippa and is now set at the top of the double staircase in the huge niche of the Belvedere palace, which houses the Pio-Clementino Museum.

181 The Gallery of Maps was decorated with maps of the various regions of Italy under the direction of the Dominican cosmographer, mathematician and architect Ignazio Danti, and painted by his brother Antonio between 1580 and 1583.

The maps were reproduced very accurately, in some cases showing the sites of the most famous battles. This decorative scheme is thus an important document of the culture and national identity of 16th-century Rome and Italy.

PIVS · IX · PONT · MAX ·
LATERITIO · PAVIMENTO
MARMOREVM · SVBSTITVIT
PONT · AN · XXXII

Vatican Museums

182 and 182-183 The architect and engineer Giuseppe Momo (1875–1940) designed many works during the first half of the 20th century. He was active in Turin and Piedmont before moving to Rome, where Pius XI commissioned him to create a staircase for the Vatican Museums and the building of the Vatican railway station. Momo's extraordinary Spiral Staircase bears witness to his style still characterized by the typical features of 19th-century eclecticism, despite being permeated by a more modern spirit.

which the famous *Apollo Belvedere* (2nd century AD) and the *Laocoon* group (1st century AD) can still be admired.

The works housed in the Pio-Clementino Museum today include the Roman replica of the famous *Apoxyomenos* by Lysippos (4th century AD) and the *Belvedere Torso* (1st century BC).

Pius VI also created the first collection of paintings in 1816, which subsequently formed the Vatican Pinacoteca, comprising works by Simone Martini, Gentile da Fabriano, Filippo Lippi, Benozzo Bozzoli, Fra Angelico, Leonardo, Titian and – among

the many masterpieces – the ten tapestries by Raphael that Leo X commissioned for the Sistine Chapel (ca. 1515) as well as Caravaggio's *Entombment* (1602-04). Gregory XVI (1831-1846) founded three important Vatican museums: the Etruscan Museum, the Egyptian Museum and the Gregorian Profane (i.e., non-religious) Museum. The Etruscan Museum opened in 1837, at a time when the extraordinary fruits of the excavation campaigns conducted at Vulci, Cerveteri and other Etrurian cities could be admired. The Egyptian Museum, inaugurated in 1839 in the wake of the enthusiasm that accompanied the opening of its forerunner in Turin, comprised tablets and inscriptions and even exhibits from Hadrian's Villa at Tivoli.

Finally, the Gregorian Profane Museum, opened in 1844, housed a collection of mainly Roman bas-reliefs, statues and mosaics. In 1854 Pius IX (1846-1878) added the Pio Christian Museum to display exhibits from the Early Christian catacombs and early Roman churches. During the papacy of Pius X (1903-1914) a section containing Hebrew inscriptions was added.

184-185 The Vatican Library was founded in 1451 by Nicholas V and completed by Sixtus IV in 1475. It brought together all the old papal libraries that had expanded over the centuries and contains manuscripts, incunabula, engravings, printed books and musical codices, palimpsests and drawings of inestimable value.

Vatican Museums

184 bottom The Chiaromonti Museum occupies part of the 1000-ft (305-m) gallery designed by Bramante between the Palace of Innocent VIII and the Vatican Palace. The New Wing (Braccio

Nuovo) built by Raffaele Stern between 1817 and 1822, is the third and last of its sections and consists of a barrel-vaulted structure with niches to house the statues.

185 The rich and colorful decoration on the vault of the Gallery of Maps was commissioned by Pope Gregory XIII (1572–85) and restored by Urban VIII (1623–44).

During the 1960s the museums founded by Gregory XVI, Pius IX and Pius X were transferred from their original premises in the Lateran Palace to a new building especially constructed for them in the Vatican; they opened to the public in 1970.

However, the importance of the Vatican Museums is not merely due to the extraordinary collections that they contain, but also to the magnificent buildings that house them, which comprise what are two of the greatest masterpieces of the Italian Renaissance: Raphael's "Stanze" and the Sistine Chapel, decorated by Michelangelo. From 1508 to his death in 1520, Raphael painted the apartment of Nicholas V for Julius II, decorating the famous Stanza della Segnatura, Stanza d'Eliodoro,

Stanza dell'Incendio and Sala di Costantino, whose complex iconographic schemes were devised by the artist and his patron. In 1508 Julius II also commissioned Michelangelo to decorate the ceiling and lunettes of the Sistine Chapel, built by Giovanni de' Dolci and inaugurated in 1493. The chapel was named after Sixtus IV, and the greatest artists of the time were summoned to decorate it, including Signorelli, Perugino, Botticelli and Ghirlandaio. Michelangelo completed this first stage of his work in 1512 and the painted scenes include the famous *Creation of Adam* in the center of the vault. In 1534 he was summoned to the Vatican by Paul III, to paint his fresco of the Last Judgment on the altar wall of the Sistine Chapel, which he completed in 1541.

186 The Chiaramonti Museum, which comprises the Corridor, Gallery of Inscriptions and New Wing, is named after its founder, Pius VII Chiaramonti, who appointed Canova as its curator.

The Corridor is divided into 60 sections and displays a rich array of statues, busts, sarcophagi and reliefs. The New Wing includes a Roman copy of the original Greek statue of the River Nile God.

Vatican Museums

186-187 The Pio-Clementino Museum, founded by Clement XIV and Pius VI, is home to a large collection of antique statuary, including the Apollo Belvedere, a Roman marble copy of the original Greek statue (AD 130–140) and the Belvedere Torso (ca 150 BC).

188-189 In 1508 Michelangelo began frescoing the ceiling of the Sistine Chapel for Julius II. The lunettes show the seven prophets and the five sibyls, while the curved part of the vault, emphasized by the classical-style architecture, is decorated with nine episodes from the Book of Genesis arranged in chronological order.

189 The Last Judgment on the wall behind the altar of the Sistine Chapel was designed and painted by Michelangelo between 1536 and 1541. It was commissioned by Clement VII (Giulio de' Medici) who died before he was able to see it finished, and completed during the papacy of Paul III (Paolo Farnese).

National Archaeological Museum

ATHENS, GREECE

The National Archaeological Museum of Athens, Greece's premier cultural institution, is the showcase for one of the world's greatest archaeological collections, and the institution has been designed to enable visitors to trace the history and admire the precious relics of ancient Greek civilization. The original nucleus of the museum's antiquities can be traced back to the French ambassador Louis Favel and the British historian George Finley and their collections of sculptures and coins. In 1813 the first step was taken towards the establishment of the museum with the foundation of the "Friends of Art Society," which not only promoted the conservation of ancient monuments, but also decided to found a museum to house exhibits and works and make them accessible to everyone. In 1824 the Society made an unsuccessful request for the collections be housed in the Erechtheum.

In 1829, the year in which Greece gained autonomy from the Ottoman Empire, and was thus able to affirm its own political and cultural identity, the Archaeological Museum was founded on the island of Aegina. It gathered together works from all over Greece, which were transferred to the Central Archaeological Museum in Athens – then housed in the ancient Temple of Hephaestus, or Theseion – in 1834. In 1837 the Archaeological Society of Athens was founded, with the aim of promoting the conservation of the country's ancient heritage and digs aimed at discovering

National Archaeological Museum

new treasures. Indeed, the Society's efforts led to important excavation campaigns, which yielded an extraordinary number of new finds.

In 1866 generous funding made it possible to commence the construction of permanent quarters, which were not completed until 1889. The building occupied a large plot donated by Helen Tositsa with the financial backing of Demetrios and Nicolaos Vernardakis, the Archaeological Society and the Greek state. The museum's original design was by the architect Ludwig Lange but his plans were subsequently modified and extended by other architects, namely Panages Kalkos, Harmodios Vlachos and Ernst Ziller. The latter was responsible for both the façade, characterized by a majestic

porch, and the central hall behind it. It is an imposing Neo-Classical building, arranged on a single story and characterized by a particularly monumental entrance. The transfer of the collections to the new museum started in 1874, but was not completed until 1878. For the first time all the antiquities from the collections of the Archaeological Society (previously housed in the Varvakeion and the Polytechneion) and from the Theseion and all the other public collections of the city were gathered together under the same roof. The museum also became home to votive sculptures from the Temple of Asclepius on the slopes of the Acropolis, tomb sculptures from the Kerameikos, and other precious pieces from Delos, Melos, Naxos, the Cyclades, Tanagra, Argos and many other provinces

192 top One of the most important rooms is dominated by the famous ancient statue known as the Poseidon of Melos, surrounded by other finds from the beautiful aegean island of Melos.

192 bottom Two of the museum's most important exhibits: the Diadoumenos of Polykleitos, found on the island of Delos, and the Horse and Jockey bronze group discovered off Cape Artemision in 1928 together with the Poseidon.

192-193 The extraordinary severe-style bronze statue known as the Poseidon of Artemision, dating from ca 460 BC, is another of the highlights of the National Archaeological Museum.

that were important centers in the development of Classical Greek culture. The new museum was originally known as the Central Museum and assumed its present name of National Archaeological Museum in April 1888. The excavations carried out over the following 50 years uncovered such an enormous number of finds that the museum immediately required more space – and extensive work was carried out between 1925 and 1939 in order to expand the premises. The east façade acquired a second story and large exhibition rooms were added. However, because of the outbreak of World War II, they never came into use.

During the second half of the 20th century architects Christos and Semni Karouzos skillfully renovated the museum, although the space was still (and remains to this day) insufficient to display the entire collection. The layout consists of four main sections: sculpture, vases and small objects, prehistoric art and bronzes. The most famous part of the museum is undoubtedly the Mycenaean secton, featuring the grave goods found in the royal tombs that the archaeologist Heinrich Schliemann uncovered in 1876. The symbol of this spectacular discovery is the so-called *Mask of Agamemnon*, a gold funerary mask dating from the 13th century BC. The museum is also home to the most famous *kouroi* and *korai* in the world, such as those by Aristion of Paros, the famous *Omphalos Apollo*, the *Eleusis Relief*, and the extraordinary bronze sculpture of Poseidon.

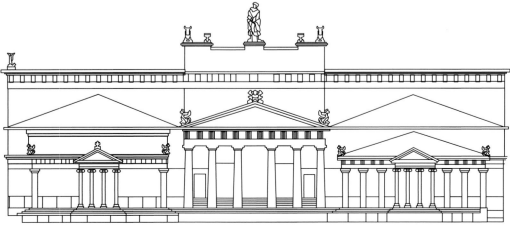

Pushkin Fine Arts Museum
MOSCOW, RUSSIA

Inaugurated in 1912, the Pushkin Museum of Fine Arts in Moscow was originally known as the Alexander III Museum of Fine Arts. Its foundation was accompanied by a solemn stone-laying ceremony attended by Czar Nicholas II (Alexander's son and successor), in the presence of the entire imperial family and the upper echelons of Muscovite society. However, the idea of establishing a museum of fine arts was conceived at the beginning of the 19th century, when two university professors, Stepan Shevyrev and Mikhail Petrovich Pogodin, presented a project to this end, decrying the lack in such an important city of an institution capable of fueling the artistic knowledge and aesthetic appreciation of the public. In the meantime two important cultural centers were established in Moscow: in 1843 the school of painting, sculpture and architecture was founded, while in 1853 the first chair of art history was established at the University of Moscow. These were, of course, fundamental achievements for the creation of a climate favorable to the birth of the museum. Ivan Tsvetaev, philologist and art historian at the University of Moscow, made an important contribution to the cause by raising funds. He managed to obtain a large donation from the wealthy magnate Yuriy Nechaev-Maltsev, a supplier of crystals to the imperial family, who also used his connections to promote and patronize the foundation of the museum. These promotional activities finally yielded sufficient funds to commence the project, and a competition was announced for the design of the building. The winner was Roman Klein, whose project was inspired by the classical architecture of ancient Greece and Rome. Indeed, he devised a sort of temple, whose façade was adorned with an Ionic colonnade, a tympanum and a classical-style frieze, which closely followed the classical canons of antiquity. The new museum was Moscow's temple of the arts and culture, and the style of its rooms varied according to the architectural styles of the periods represented in the collections.

In accordance with the intentions of Professor Tsvetaev, who

had conceived the museum as a study and research center connected to the university, one of the first collections to be housed in the museum was that of plaster casts of masterpieces of ancient art, which still constitutes one of the most fascinating and important sections today. The museum was built between 1898 and 1912, when it was officially opened as the Alexander III Museum of Fine Arts (it did not assume its current name until 1937). The collections were subsequently expanded, this time with original masterpieces. In 1909 the museum purchased the collection of Oriental and Egyptian art of V.S. Golinishev, a

194-195 and 194 bottom
The competition announced in 1896 for the design of the Pushkin Museum in Moscow was won by Muscovite architect Roman Klein (1858– 1924), whose project was inspired by the classical

architecture of ancient Greece and Rome. The museum, officially opened to the public in 1912, was conceived as a temple and its façade was adorned with an Ionic colonnade, a tympanum and a classical-style frieze.

195 Outside the building stands one of the versions of The Thinker, the famous statue by French sculptor Auguste Rodin (1840–1917), originally

conceived to crown the ensemble for the Gates of Hell, commissioned in 1880 for the Museum of Decorative Arts in Paris.

Pushkin Fine Arts Museum

196 and 197 The Pushkin Museum was inaugurated by Nicholas II shortly before the tragic end of the Romanov dynasty. Its layout is rather solemn and highly evocative, due to the individual decoration of its rooms, which echo the provenance of their contents. Between 1941 and 1944 most of the museum's collection was moved to Siberia to save it from destruction. This proved to be a wise precaution, for although Moscow was not taken by the Germans, the museum suffered serious bomb damage.

Pushkin Fine Arts Museum

198 top The Pushkin Museum's collection of ancient art comprises over 1000 pieces, including jewelry, sculpture and artifacts of all kinds, ranging from ancient Egypt to Greece and Rome, and was pieced together during campaigns conducted by the museum.

198 bottom The Pushkin Museum's first exhibits of ancient art came from the collection formerly housed in Cabinet of Fine Arts and Antiquities of Moscow University, which initially consisted mainly of plaster casts but was later expanded

with original works of antique art. The extraordinary collection of ancient Greek pottery, on the other hand, was transferred to the museum in 1929 from the collections of the History Museum and Museum of Ceramics, the Tretyakov Gallery and the Rumyantsev Museum.

199 Roman Klein scrupulously followed the canons of classical Greek architecture (or at least as they were perceived during his time). His rooms are modeled on Hellenistic temple architecture, implicitly enhancing the value of the artworks housed within.

famous St. Petersburg scholar, and during the same period a collection of Italian art dating from the 12th to the 14th century was donated by M.S. Shchekin, the Russian consul in Trieste. The museum's collections grew even more remarkably over the subsequent years, even during the Russian Revolution, due to the cultural policy that imposed the nationalization of privately owned works of art. The museum thus became home to other important collections from all over Russia, which were joined in the 1930's by those from the Hermitage in St. Petersburg and from the Museum of Modern Western Art. However, while the Pushkin Museum is home to the collections of important Russian noble families, its greatness also stems from the non-aristocratic collectors whose treasures it houses. Following World War I the museum also promoted and popularized

Russian avant-garde art, organizing important temporary exhibitions dedicated to contemporary artistic movements. However, 1937 was a difficult year, for it marked the onset of Stalin's Great Purge and was accompanied by an enormous loss of national intellectual and political resources. In order to commemorate these losses, the museum was dedicated to the poet Alesksandr Pushkin, who had died exactly 100 years earlier.

Today the museum's famous plaster casts and ancient Egyptian artifacts are flanked by one of the world's greatest collections of European art, featuring works by important 17th- and 18th-century Italian, Dutch, Flemish, Spanish and French artists, and numerous late 19th-century French masterpieces. The museum also houses a large collection of decorative and applied arts and collections of coins and medals, prints and drawings.

The Hermitage
ST. PETERSBURG, RUSSIA

Although its name may bring to mind a single building, the famous and magnificent State Hermitage in St. Petersburg actually comprises six sumptuous edifices situated on near the Neva River: the Winter Palace, the Small Hermitage, the Large Hermitage, the New Hermitage, the Theater and the Menshikov Palace. Constructed between the 18th and 19th centuries, these buildings form a well-balanced complex, despite their different styles. The origins of this unique architectural group date back to 1754-62, when Empress Elizabeth commissioned architect Francesco Bartolomeo Rastrelli to build the Winter Palace as the residence of the Czars. The scale of the work was so impressive as to absorb all the timber and stone resources of the area of Lake Ladoga for three years, but the result was an architectural gem.

The building, in Russian Baroque style, is magnificent by any standard and seems to change according to the viewpoint of the observer, due to the different composition of the volumes and decoration of its façades, marked by elegant orders of columns with Corinthian capitals. It was next to the Winter Palace (whose 3 floors house over 1000 rooms) that Catherine the Great ordered the constructiono of a "retreat" in 1764. The new building was envisaged as a secluded and secure place where a few select guests could admire and enjoy the works of art that the empress had started to collect. The museum's true founder was thus Catherine the Great, who was the first to conceive its function, albeit originally restricted to an elite public. The empress gathered together an astounding number of private collections, based on a wide variety of exhibits – ranging from curiosities from the animal and vegetable kingdoms to works of art – and displayed them in the Hanging Garden and in the "exhibition" galleries. They included the collection of Dutch and Flemish paintings that had belonged to Johann Ernst Gotzkowsky; that of the Parisian banker Pierre Crozat, with works by Titian, Giorgione, Raphael and Veronese and other great masters, including Rembrandt and Rubens; the

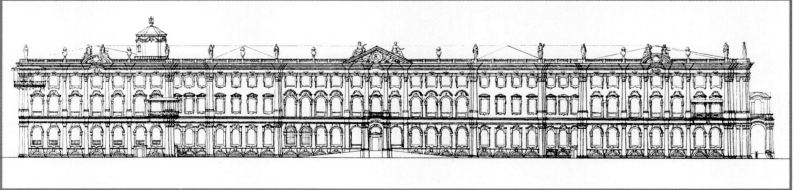

200-201 and 201 bottom
The Hermitage in St. Petersburg
was founded by Catherine the
Great, who in 1764 ordered the
construction of a "retreat" (a
hermitage) next to the czars'
sumptuous Winter Palace, built
by Francesco Bartolomeo Rastrelli
between 1754 and 1762.

200 bottom The Winter Palace
(1754–62) overlooks the huge
Palace Square. Its façade is
characterized by a three-arched
entrance and a double order of
half columns and richly decorated
windows. The two-story building
has a square plan around a large
inner courtyard and was designed
by Francesco Bartolomeo
Rastrelli.

The Hermitage

202 A series of double columns characterizes the façade of the Winter Palace that overlooks the huge Palace Square, dominated by the monumental Alexander Column. Each of the gates is adorned with a gilded two-headed eagle, the heraldic device of the Byzantine emperors, later adopted by the Czars of Russia and Peter the Great.

202-203 The façade of the New Hermitage (1839–51), designed by Franz Karl Leo von Klenze and built by Vasily Stasov and Nikolai Yefimov, features an imposing portico supported by ten 16-ft (5-m) tall gray granite atlantes by the sculptor Alexander Terebenev, which were inspired by the Porch of the Caryatids of the Erechtheum of the Acropolis in Athens.

Coblentz collection, comprising over 6,000 drawings; the collection of Count von Brühl, featuring works by Cranach, Tiepolo and Bellotto, the entire Walpole collection at Houghton Hall of about 200 Flemish and Dutch paintings; and the Boudoin collection, with works by Van Dyck and Rembrandt. At the empress' death in 1796, the Hermitage collection boasted almost 4000 works of art, and a new building – the Large Hermitage, designed by Yuri Velten – had already been erected to house them all in 1771-87. Although it had three stories in order to connect it to the existing buildings, it is far more sober in style, reflecting the classicizing spirit of the period. In 1792 Giacomo Quarenghi built a new wing for the Large Hermitage, connecting it to the Small Hermitage and the Theater.

The enormous artistic heritage housed in this constantly

growing complex long remained a private collection and was not opened to the public until 1805, when its management became partially independent, although remaining under imperial control. The successors of Catherine the Great, particularly her grandson Alexander I, also added to her remarkable legacy, and during the 19th century the collection was made more representative of the various European schools with acquisitions including a huge collection of Spanish paintings, the Barbarigo Venetian collection and that of the Dutch King William II. Between 1839 and 1851 the need for more space resulted in the construction of the New Hermitage, which was inaugurated in 1852. The building was designed by the architect Franz Karl Leo von Klenze to complement the Winter Palace. The New Hermitage was the first building expressly and solely constructed to house the museum's

collections and is the most sedate edifice of the entire complex. Although monumental, its architecture is extremely well balanced and it constitutes an excellent example of 19th-century eclecticism and historicism, for it was inspired by the historical evolution of tastes and techniques, employing a mixture of classical, Renaissance and Baroque elements.

During the 19th century the Hermitage experienced various ups and downs, but following the sale of numerous works under Nicholas I, a new golden period commenced, which reached its height following the October Revolution. Indeed, after 1917 private collections were nationalized, resulting in the addition of many collections confiscated from the imperial palaces, and the Hermitage was officially declared a state museum. During the 20th century, this huge artistic heritage was further enriched with

several collections from the State Museum of New Western Art in Moscow, which was closed in 1948, and its chronological scope was extended to modern art, with works by Picasso, Matisse, Van Gogh, Cézanne and Gauguin. The Hermitage owes part of its international renown to its famous Treasure Gallery, housing extraordinary collections of antiquities and decorative arts, and to its archaeological collections, which span a period stretching from prehistoric times to the classical Greco-Roman and Oriental civilizations. It is also home to a very interesting collection of weapons and armor commenced by Nicholas I, a numismatic section, a section dedicated to the decorative arts, and a porcelain museum, in addition to a large section curated by the Russian Department of Culture, which houses over 30,000 exhibits including a precious collection of icons.

The Hermitage

204 In 1783 Catherine II commissioned Giacomo Quarenghi to create a reconstruction of the Raphael Loggias of the Vatican Palace in Rome.

205 top The Hermitage's art collection is traditionally dated from 1764, when Catherine II bought the collection of 225 paintings belonging to Johann Ernst Gotzkowsky.

205 bottom Situated in what is now the entrance hall of the Hermitage Museum, the Ambassadors' Staircase was damaged in the fire of 1837 and rebuilt by Vasily Stasov according to Rastrelli's design.

The Hermitage

206 top The photograph clearly reveals the classical inspiration underlying the mid 18th-century decoration of the Pavilion Hall, in which references to classical Greek and Roman antiquity merge with Renaissance and Moorish themes to form an eclectic blend.

206 center The ground floor of the New Hermitage houses the collection of antique art commenced by Peter the Great. These rooms alternate monumental features inspired by Greek and Roman art and the eclectic decoration typical of the 19th century.

206 bottom The Majolica Room includes famous works by Raphael.

206-207 Visiting the galleries today, it is hard to believe that they were used as air-raid shelters little more than 60 years ago.

208-209 The large and magnificent Pavilion Hall (ca 1850) was decorated by Andrei Stackenschneider in typical eclectic style inspired by Renaissance architectural models mixed with Moorish motifs.

210-211 The Great Hall, also known as the Nicholas Hall, has an area of ca 12,000 sq. ft (1115 sq. m), making it one of the largest rooms of the Winter Palace. It was designed during the 18th century by Giacomo Quarenghi and is currently used to host temporary exhibitions.

210 bottom left The church is one of the buildings that was subsequently added to the main complex of the Winter Palace and is topped by a large gold dome that marks its location between Palace Square and the adjoining Small Hermitage.

The Hermitage

210 bottom right The private apartments include those of Czarina Maria Aleksandrovna, the wife of Alexander II, with the rococo music room decorated by architect Gerald Bosset with Louis XV-style furnishings.

211 top The Throne Room of Peter the Great is dedicated to the first Czar of Russia. The central niche houses Jacopo Amiconi's painting of Peter the Great with Minerva and the silver throne made by Nicholas Clausen for the Czarina Anna Ivanovna.

211 bottom Alexander Brullov's decoration of the Gold Room (1838) was inspired by the architecture of several rooms of the Kremlin in Moscow. It was part of the private apartments of Alexandra Feodorovna, wife of Czar Nicholas I.

212 top and 212-213 The walls of the War Gallery (1812–26) are adorned with the portraits of over 100 generals who distinguished themselves on the battlefield during the Russian army's four great victories over the French.

212 center and bottom The rich collection of modern paintings is housed on the second floor of the Winter Palace and comprises 20th-century works defined by the Soviet regime as "ideologically harmful." Most of these works are from the collections of Sergei Shchukin and the Morozov brothers, and from the State Museum of Modern Western Art, which was closed in 1948.

The Hermitage

214-215 and 214 bottom The Egyptian Museum in Cairo is an outgrowth of the Egyptian Antiquities Service, established in 1835. It was designed in Neoclassical style by French architect Marcel Dourgnon and houses the most comprehensive collection of ancient Egyptian antiquities in the world, with over 130,000 pieces on display and thousands of other artifacts in its storerooms.

Egyptian Museum
CAIRO, EGYPT

The Egyptian Museum in Cairo, with its extraordinary collections documenting 5000 years of Egyptian history and civilization, represents a major effort to stem the dispersion of the nation's priceless artistic heritage. Napoleon's invasion of Egypt in 1798 and the subsequent publication of illustrated works on Ancient Egypt's fascinating and evocative civilization fired the interest of curators and collectors throughout the world. The invasion and the subsequent British and French colonialism led to the expatriation of many of the country's precious artifacts, particularly during the 19th and early 20th centuries.

A growing awareness that numerous exceptionally rich collections of ancient Egyptian art had been assembled in other countries and that local authorities had not developed any effective legislation to control and protect the nation's cultural heritage led to action. In 1835 the Egyptian government established the Egyptian Antiquities Service, creating a collection that was initially housed in the Azbakian Garden but later transferred to Saladin's Citadel.

However, the driving force behind the museum's actual foundation was the French archaeologist Auguste Mariette, Assistant Conservator at the Department of Egyptian Art at the Louvre, who had led several important excavation campaigns in Egypt. Realizing the precarious situation of Egypt's artistic heritage, Mariette began the painstaking but fruitful task of surveying and documenting all the ruins in an attempt to preserve them for the nation. He transferred assembled many of the objects uncovered during the digs to a warehouse next to the disused offices of a shipping company. These were situated on the bank of the Nile at Bulaq, and here, in 1858, the first museum was founded in a building formerly used as a steamship depot.

The collections were initially arranged in rooms frescoed by Mariette himself, but more space was soon required and the structure was extended in 1863. However, the Nile's flooding constantly threatened the site, making the premises unsuitable. Consequently, it was decided to build a proper museum that was larger and more representative of Egypt's great past.

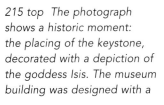

215 top The photograph shows a historic moment: the placing of the keystone, decorated with a depiction of the goddess Isis. The museum building was designed with a T-shaped plan, to simplify future extension and the collocation of the most imposing monuments in the central atrium, with the smaller exhibits housed in the wings.

216-217 The ground-floor atrium, which houses part of the of the museum's statuary collection, is dominated by the seated colossi of the king Amenhotep III and his wife Tiy (14th century BC). The construction of the building commenced in 1897 and the museum opened to the public in 1902, at the end of the period of Ottoman rule in Egypt. The two-story building has around 100 rooms that house the most awe-inspiring and rare collection of Egyptian antiquities in the world.

217 Beneath the cupola, a gallery runs around the entrance hall of the museum, which is visited by millions of people each year.

Egyptian Museum

Construction commenced in 1897 on the orders of the khedive of Egypt, Abbas Hilmi Pasha. The building, situated in the heart of Cairo, was designed in Neo-Classical style by the French architect Marcel Dourgnon, and was opened to the public on November 15, 1902. Its T-shaped plan was chosen to aid the circulation of visitors, while the large atrium was designed to provide the perfect setting for the colossal stone figures of Pharaoh Amenhotep III and his wife and the breathtaking statue of Ramesses II.

Mariette died in 1881, before he had the chance to see his hopes accomplished. However, the Egyptian government commemorated him with a mausoleum in the museum courtyard and a bronze statue. This was placed among the busts of pioneering scholars and archaeologists in Egyptology, whose studies and research have contributed to our knowledge of the history and culture of the ancient civilizations of the Nile Valley.

Pre-eminent among the museum's most famous and precious treasures are the magnificent artifacts from the young Pharaoh Tutankhamon's tomb, which Howard Carter discovered in the Valley of the Kings in 1922. Visitors can admire the jeweled gold funerary mask, richly decorated alabaster Canopic jars, the gilded wooden throne studded with jewels and glass paste, the precious gold and silver pectoral, and the wooden statue of the god Anubis. All these outstanding items come from the tomb of this 18th-Dynasty pharaoh, whose short reign lasted about ten years.

The Egyptian Museum also houses the tomb furnishings of Thutmose II, Thutmose III, Amenhotep III and Horemheb. In addition to the particularly evocative Royal Mummy Room, containing around 30 royal mummies, the museum also houses many exhibits from the tombs of Tanis (a city in the Nile delta) and artifacts from the city of Thebes, including the extraordinary Book of the Dead, written on remarkably well-preserved papyrus.

Yad Vashem Museum

JERUSALEM, ISRAEL

Yad Vashem in a Jerusalem is both a museum and a moving memorial to the terrible history of the Holocaust, the six million Jews murdered by the Nazis, and the heroes who tried to stop the genocide, often risking their own lives in the process. The museum, whose name is derived from a verse in the Book of Isaiah and means "a memorial and a name," was established in 1953 through the Memorial Law passed by the Knesset, Israel's Parliament.

The historical museum complex is part of a huge area that is also home to a synagogue, an art gallery, many monuments and open-air works of art, all dedicated to the theme of memorial and commemoration. The museum was designed by the Israeli architect Moshe Safdie, with the dual aim of creating a striking building, characterized by a coherent narrative and educational layout designed to recount and commemorate the historical events regarding the Holocaust, and a place intended to touch the visitor emotionally. In his design Safdie tries to strike a sensitive balance between the aspects of a museum and spiritual contemplation typical of a memorial.

In addition to the many detailed sections housing historical exhibits and reconstructions, Yad Vashem also features various other structures that make it the most

218 top, bottom and 218-219
Two aerial views of the complex,
showing the Square of Hope, with
olive trees, the long building of
the Holocaust History Museum
and the cylindrical Hall of Names
beyond.

219 bottom left Moshe Safdie
designed a concrete building that
cuts through the landscape with a
long underground corridor around
which the exhibition halls are
arranged, covering an area of over
180,000 sq. ft (16,725 sq. m).

219 bottom right Memorial
ceremonies are held in the
solemn Hall of Remembrance,
whose floor is engraved with
the names of the 22 main Nazi
concentration camps located
throughout Europe.

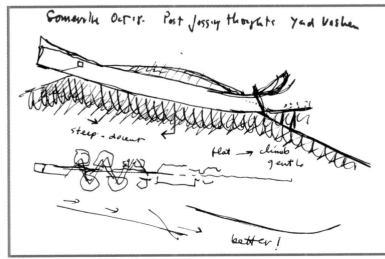

Yad Vashem Museum

220 The tragedy of the Holocaust and the cultural context in which it occurred are recounted through reconstructions, photographs, archival documents, letters, personal items, films and video projections in the evocative underground rooms of the museum. Several small rooms, delimited by concrete walls, are characterized by semidarkness, which is necessary for the artificially lit installations and multimedia presentations.

221 The corridor with converging walls presents intense fragments of 20th-century history. Visitors progress through the darkest underground parts of the museum before reaching the light at the exit, with its splendid view over the city.

important center of Holocaust studies and documentation in the world. Since the 1950s, and particularly since 1992, it has been engaged not only in the historical reconstruction of these dramatic events, but also in collecting the names of the victims of the concentration camps. Today, with the powerful aid of the Internet, it is possible for any individual to contribute to the database accessible through the museum's website by sending the names and personal data of the unidentified victims in the archive's list, of whom there are still around three million.

The complex blends perfectly with the area and the view of Jerusalem. Parts of the triangular building are carved into the mountain on which it stood. The museum has a long underground walkway, which starts and ends outside. This design was partly dictated by the need to create underground rooms and passages as the ideal setting for various multimedia installations featuring films, videos, projections and exhibitions of photographs, along with the display of moving exhibits such as diaries, letters and objects that belonged to the victims. However, the underground paths are also highly

222, 223 and 224-225 The Hall of Names is one of the most moving and evocative parts of Yad Vashem. The room is formed by two conical structures: an upper one, reaching skywards, and an opposing one carved out of the floor and filled with water. Visitors can contemplate the photographs of the Holocaust on the ceiling formed by the upper cone from a circular platform beneath it, while the portraits reflected in the clear water evoke the many unnamed victims.

Yad Vashem Museum

effective metaphors of a possible journey back in time, to a difficult and particularly dark moment in the history of humankind.

The entire museum structure is made from concrete. It has a symbolic meaning: it is a material that cannot be destroyed or damaged, just as the memory of the horrific extermination carried out by the Nazis must never be diminished or destroyed. The avenue leading to the museum is lined with some 200 trees dedicated to the Righteous Among the Nations: the heroes who tried to stop the genocide. The exhibition itinerary includes a 600-foot tunnel in the mountainside, which leads to the Hall of Remembrance, at the center of which an eternal flame burns and whose floor is engraved with the names of the Nazi regime's 22 main concentration camps. However, the focus of the entire complex is the very moving Hall of Names. This is the most

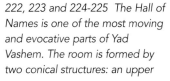

evocative and emotionally powerful part of the memorial. It houses two conical structures: the ceiling is formed by a 33-ft (10-m) high cone, while an opposing cone carved out of the rock of the floor is filled with water.

From the circular platform beneath the upper cone visitors can observe the true repository of memory: indeed, the walls of the ceiling cone are covered with some 600 photographs of the victims of the Holocaust, reflected in the water below, recalling the many martyrs who have never been identified but are commemorated in the circular walls of the room, where there are numerous gaps in the six million spaces dedicated to the Pages of Testimony. After having paused in this room, visitors continue the itinerary to emerge in the light and the present, in a spot offering a magnificent view of Jerusalem, the modern and complex heart of the Holy Land.

Tokyo National Museum

TOKYO, JAPAN

The Tokyo National Museum is home to the world's most precious collections of Japanese art, but it also dedicates great space and attention to art from other regions of the East. It is a relatively recent museum complex composed of three main structures: the museum, which was rebuilt after the 1923 earthquake on occasion of the coronation of the crown prince; the Hyokeikan, designed by Toma Kitatayama and built in 1908 to celebrate the wedding of the crown prince; and the newest part, the Gallery of Horyuji Treasures. The National Museum also has huge gardens containing other buildings of great historical and artistic interest, such as the Okyokan and the Kujokan, and the Tengo-an and Shunsoro teahouses, in addition to buildings housing conference halls, a library and an auditorium.

The first Japanese museum, and nucleus of today's National Museum, was established in 1871 in the Taiseiden Hall of the former Seido (Confucian temple) at Yushima, Tokyo. Japan's acquaintance with Europe and its many rapidly growing cultural institutions and museums led it to place greater emphasis on both the protection and display of its own heritage. Consequently the Yushima Museum, whose large collection of artistic and scientific exhibits was already starting to require more space, was moved to Uchiyamashita-cho, where it remained until 1882. Finally, the collections were moved to Ueno Park, where they were housed in the art gallery built by the British architect Josiah Conder for the Second National Industrial Exhibition in 1881.

During this early period the museum's main purpose was closely associated with trade shows; the Ministry of Agriculture and Commerce, under whose authority it was placed, saw it as a useful tool for stimulating production. In 1886 control of the museum was transferred to the Ministry of the Imperial

226 The large garden surrounding the buildings of the Tokyo National Museum also bears witness to traditional Japanese culture and "natural architecture", with a variety of plants that mark the passage of the seasons, such as flowering cherry trees, and is home to five typical ceremonial teahouses.

226-227 The Main Gallery is known as the Honkan and houses the core of the museum's collection of Japanese art. The original building was designed by British architect Josiah Conder, but was damaged in the Great Kanto Earthquake of 1923. The present building was designed by Watanabe Jin and built in 1932–38.

Household, which placed greater emphasis on the museum's cultural role connected with the study and popularization of Japanese art history, which further boosted its growing prestige around the turn of the century. In 1909 the Hyokeikan ("Gallery to Express Congratulations"), built to commemorate the wedding of the crown prince (who later became Emperor Taisho), was opened. But disaster also struck: in 1923 a powerful earthquake completely destroyed the main block of the museum, which was entirely rebuilt and reopened in 1938.

In the meantime, the mainly artistic focus of the museum led to the transfer of the collections of the Natural Products Department to the current National Science Museum in Tokyo. In 1947 a new Constitution was established and the Imperial Household Museum was placed under the authority of the Ministry of Education and renamed the National Museum. Its educational role was further strengthened in 1950, the year in which the law for Protection of Cultural Properties was passed. During this period a new gallery, the Horyuji Homotsukan, was added to the museum and inaugurated in 1964.

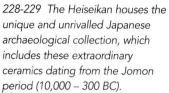

Tokyo National Museum

228-229 The Heiseikan houses the unique and unrivalled Japanese archaeological collection, which includes these extraordinary ceramics dating from the Jomon period (10,000 – 300 BC).

228 bottom left The museum's collection of Japanese art, featuring various types of exhibits, is displayed in the Honkan building, in 24 exhibition rooms on two floors.

228 bottom right The Toyokan is the museum's Asian gallery and was designed by architect Taniguchi Yoshiro. It was opened in 1968 and consists of ten rooms arranged in a spiral on three levels.

229 The museum's rooms and functional structures are the interesting result of the combination of Western grandeur and traditional Japanese linearity and horizontality.

It was designed to house the splendid treasures donated to the Imperial Household by the Horyuji temple in 1878. The temple itself was subsequently renovated and reopened in 1999.

The Tokyo National Museum is divided into sections on the basis of the materials of the exhibits and subdivided into collections of archaeology, textiles, metals, weapons, ceramics, lacquer ware, paintings, sculpture and calligraphy. It houses and displays over 100,000 objects, chiefly from important donations by the Imperial Household, private gifts and exchanges with important international museums, skillfully arranged to form as complete a picture as possible of all the

most important stages in Japanese art, its patronage and its contamination with Oriental art in general.

The collection of Chinese art comprises many exhibits covering a period extending from the late Neolithic to the Yuan (1279-1368) and Ming (1368-1644) periods. The museum also has a particularly fine section dedicated to painting, which houses many extraordinary kakemonos (hanging ink-and-brush paintings on paper or silk scrolls). Other works of art in the huge Japanese painting section include the famous series of Heian-period screens with scenes illustrating the life of the famous Prince Shotoku Taishi (574-622), and precious works depicting religious subjects and saints.

*230-231 and 230 bottom
The immense variety and richness
of Asian art prompted the Art
Gallery of New South Wales in
Sydney to extend its premises
with a new structure that added*

*a further 7500 sq. ft (700 sq. m)
of display space. The overall
impression created by the
architecture is one of great
lightness and harmony. Both
of these qualities are highly*

*esteemed in the artistic traditions
of Asia, and Japan in particular.
Indeed, Japanese art forms the
core of the museum's collection,
which dates back to the late
19th century.*

*231 The details of the
architecture also evoke Far-
Eastern themes, such as this
metal lotus flower, which performs
both a decorative and a structural
function.*

AGNSW New Asian Galleries

SYDNEY, AUSTRALIA

The new Asian galleries of the Art Gallery of New South Wales in Sydney are the pleasing result of a recent and extremely fascinating extension of the existing premises. The Gallery's Asian collection, which comprises extraordinary pieces of ancient art, originated in 1879, when Government of Japan made a gift of a large group of ceramics and bronzes to New South Wales. Almost a century later, in 1972, New South Wales decided to open a small gallery dedicated to Asian art to house this core collection. The Australian architect Walter Liberty Vernon designed the original building, but in 1988 the display area was expanded with the addition of concrete and glass wings designed by Andrew Anderson. In the meantime private individuals had swelled the collection with many generous donations. Perhaps the most famous and extensive of these was that made in 1962 by the collector Sydney Cooper, which added many examples of ceramics and votive sculptures to the already large collection.

The curatorial department entrusted with the study and organization of the collection was officially established in 1979 and, under the direction of Jackie Menzies, commenced important and in-depth research and programs aimed at popularizing the history, culture and art of ancient Asian civilizations. Then, as now, the collection was made up of a great variety of artifacts, including numerous types of Chinese porcelain and ceramics, an extensive selection of Ming period (1368-1644) and Qing period (1644-1912) paintings, modern paintings, Japanese screens with rich gold-leaf backgrounds, Buddhist art, Indian sculptures and extraordinary examples of Southeast Asian textile art. Its many exceptional sections, which make it Australia's most important Asian art gallery, allow visitors to approach and discover Oriental cultures and traditions, illustrated with works of art from antiquity through to the present day.

The amazing new extension, which has added 7500 sq. ft (700 sq. m) of space, was designed by Richard Johnson of the Johnson Pilton Walker architectural firm. The structure not only has a strong visual impact, but also a great symbolic significance, for the white glass and steel cube appears to float on top of the original building, pivoted on stainless steel lotus flowers. The architect's inspiration for the project came from the intriguing and highly evocative image of the lantern, which is a recurrent symbol in Asian cultures. The new structure has two floors, used chiefly for temporary exhibitions.

The layout of the Asian galleries, divided into sections on the basis of the geographical provenance of the artifacts, allows visitors to admire and understand the countless cultural differences that have characterized the vast continent, from ancient times to the present day.

232-233 and 232 bottom
The interior of the museum has two large well-lit floors with areas dedicated to temporary exhibitions on both. The extension was designed by Andrew Anderson, who specializes in this kind of work. The installation of the ventilation system proved particularly tricky, requiring the construction of an attic among the beams of the building.

AGNSW
New Asian Galleries

The various sections are dedicated to themes such as Asian religions, featuring extraordinary examples of Buddhist and Hindu votive art, and export ceramics, illustrating the ancient network of sea routes that conveyed artifacts from China, Thailand and Vietnam to Japan, the Philippines, Indonesia and India. Remarkable sections are dedicated to Indian, Korean and Vietnamese art, but the largest and richest ones of all are those of Chinese and Japanese art.

The Chinese section contains ritual bronzes dating from the Shang (ca. 1766-1060 BC) and Zhou (1122-256) BC) dynasties, Tang funerary sculptures, splendid ceramics that document 7000 years of Chinese culture, and paintings, landscapes and prints covering a period from antiquity to the present day.

The Japanese section features a fascinating part illustrating the art of the samurai, with ceremonial objects and garments, along with ceramics and, above all, the magnificent paintings of the Edo (or Tokugawa) period, from 1603 to 1867.

233 Special materials and sealing systems were used in order to minimize the noise from a nearby freeway, ensuring the essential tranquility required to appreciate the gallery's collections. The two floors of the building are used to stage exhibitions of ancient and contemporary art. The ground floor is dedicated to the Far East, with works from China, Japan and Korea, while the first floor is home to works of sacred art and exhibits documenting Southeast Asian artistic traditions.

AGNSW New Asian Galleries

234-235 Natural light, filtered through the large glazed surfaces, partially penetrates the foyer, thus ensuring that the exhibition areas and other public spaces of the galleries are not completely isolated. The construction of the new wing was timed to coincide with the Sydney Olympic Games and the centenary of the Australian Federation.

National Gallery of Victoria
MELBOURNE, AUSTRALIA

The National Gallery of Victoria (NGV) is Australia's largest and oldest art gallery. It was founded in 1861, during the ten-year period in which the state of Victoria was a self-governing British colony with Melbourne as its capital, hence the "National" its name. Although Victoria was a fairly small state, it was densely populated and industrialized, due to the gold rush that followed the discovery of the precious metal near Melbourne in 1851, the year in which it was declared a colony. During the same decade the city's size, population density and economic importance increased dramatically. The NGV's fortunes are connected with this moment of prosperity and wealth. Indeed, it was the generous donation of a famous rich industrialist, Alfred Felton, that permitted the acquisition of the first works – both old and modern – that constituted the initial step toward the foundation and growth of the gallery. The collections originally focused on Australian and Aboriginal art, but gradually came to encompass a growing number of international works. The gallery's collections are currently split between two different buildings: the historic premises in St Kilda Road are home to NGV International, featuring the permanent collection of international works, while the more recent Ian Potter Centre in Federation Square houses NGV Australia, which comprises the Australian and Aboriginal works.

236 top Visitors to the National Gallery of Victoria are greeted by its long façade on St Kilda Road. The building is clad with bluestone, a type of dolerite that was widely used in Melbourne during the mid 19th century.

236 center and bottom The renovation of the museum during the 1990s transformed the original complex by George Grounds, built in 1859–68, while maintaining its fundamental characteristics.

237 This view of the museum shows the spire of the Arts Centre (at the top of the photograph), also designed by George Grounds, and the circular Hamer Hall. The Ian Potter Center can be seen in the center of the photograph.

During the 1990s an architecture competition was held to redesign the exhibition area of the main premises in St Kilda Road. The goal of the competition was to successfully address display needs and improve public access and use of the structure. The Italian architect Mario Bellini won the competition, defeating several famous adversaries including Gae Aulenti, Arata Isozaki and Ieoh Ming Pei. Bellini's project respected the existing structure, built in 1968, and the value that it had assumed for the local population, despite making considerable changes to the building with the use of avant-garde materials and technologies.

Instead of rebuilding the premises in the true sense of the word, Bellini extended them, reinventing and reworking the spaces, which he modified chiefly from the inside, while ensuring continuity with the past by maintaining the bluish-gray color of the bluestone exterior. The interior features three courtyards, including a large central one with a spectacular glass roof, and some 30 rooms for the display of the permanent collection. These house works ranging from Egyptian, Greco-Roman and Asian antiquities through to a representative section dedicated to contemporary art. In addition to the huge entrance hall, areas for educational activities, and rooms for performances, conferences and lectures, Mario Bellini and his team also designed three large display areas devised to house temporary exhibitions.

National Gallery of Victoria

239 The NGV complex comprises galleries dedicated to the art of all the continents, as well as an auditorium and other facilities, such as a restaurant. The continuous expansion of the collection (which comprised 60,000 works in 2006) required the construction of a new building. Consequently, the Ian Potter Center was erected a few hundred feet north of the main gallery, which is now known as the NGV International.

In terms of layout, paths were created with different colors to distinguish each section in order to help visitors orient themselves among the various collections.

The National Gallery displays many collections, but the most representative ones are undoubtedly those that recount local history. These are housed in the Ian Potter Centre and include a collection of Aboriginal art produced by the native Kulin population and the Torres Strait Islanders, along with many works by artists of the Heidelberg School, the late 19th-century Australian art movement that focused mainly on the depiction of local landscapes.

Another important attraction is the Joseph Brown Collection of Australian works that the collector and art dealer of that name donated to the NGV in 2004. It is the largest collection ever donated to the gallery, consisting of some 450 works, including paintings, sculptures, engravings and drawings dating from the colonial period to the present.

The many works of the International Collection housed in St Kilda Road include The Banquet of Cleopatra by Giovanni Battista Tiepolo, about 180 drawings by Albrecht Dürer, and paintings by Paolo Veronese, Gianlorenzo Bernini, William Blake, Nicolas Poussin, Camille Pissarro, Jean-Baptiste-Camille Corot, John Constable, Robert Delaunay, Balthus and Francis Bacon.

National Gallery of Canada

OTTAWA, CANADA

The National Gallery of Canada, in Ottawa boasts a long history and tradition. Its collections comprise numerous works of art from all over the world and from all periods, making it the most important and representative gallery in Canada. It was founded in 1880, when Canada's Governor General John Douglas Sutherland Campbell, Marquess of Lorne, inaugurated the Royal Canadian Academy's first official exhibition at the Clarendon Hotel in Ottawa, the gallery's first temporary home.

Before moving to its current splendid building, the National Gallery of Canada occupied a series of temporary premises, commencing in 1882 when the works were transferred from the Clarendon Hotel to a remodeled two-room workshop situated on Parliament Hill. In 1888 the National Gallery was transferred to rooms in O'Connor Street, where it remained until 1911, when it moved to the third floor of the Victoria Memorial Museum in Metcalfe Street. In 1952 an architecture competition was announced to design a new and more practical gallery building to be erected in Cartier Square. However, the competition was stopped in 1954, and in 1959 the Governor General Vincent Massey laid the cornerstone of the Lorne Building, where the entire collection was transferred in 1960.

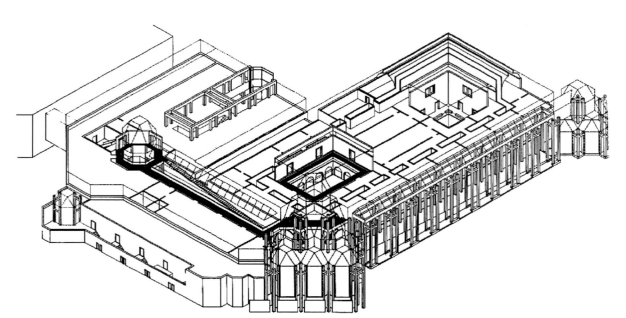

240-241 and 241 bottom Moshe Safdie designed the National Gallery of Canada in Ottawa in a style that recalls the city's Gothic Revival architecture. His building echoes the majestic beauty of the spires and domes of the Library of Parliament and the Notre-Dame Cathedral Basilica, reproposing their forms in different materials, and thus creating new effects.

240 bottom The National Gallery of Canada is housed in a large and stately building built between 1983 and 1989. It has an L-shaped plan arranged on three floors, including a basement.

242 Light is entrusted with the task of expanding and defining the volumes of the museum, by day and by night. Safdie's almost ethereal design masterly substitutes both the visual and the decorative function of the structure, shaping a building that is completed integrated with its surroundings.

243 This close-up of the glass spire above the Great Hall reveals the juxtaposition of shapes and light that suggests parallels between the building of the National Gallery of Canada and Gothic architecture. However, the extensive use of glass and steel frames has allowed the style to be remodeled, resulting in a lightweight building flooded with natural light.

National Gallery of Canada

244 The entire complex covers an area of over 500,000 sq. ft (46,450 sq. m), of which ca 135,000 (12,540 sq. m) house the collection, while the remainder *consist of huge, evocative public areas. Indeed, the architect's intention was to create a sort of modern cathedral in terms of both appearance and function.* *245 One of the most evocative areas of the museum is the long corridor, punctuated by imposing columns, which draws visitors toward the Great Hall.*

National Gallery of Canada

However, the turning point came in 1983, when Moshe Safdie was commissioned to design the striking building that houses the National Gallery today. Construction commenced in 1984 and the gallery reopened to the public on March 8, 1988, on a sort of promontory overlooking the Ottawa River at its junction with the Rideau Canal.

The building materials (mainly glass, steel and rose granite) give the structure the light, yet majestic and captivating, appearance of a modern cathedral with a long L-shaped plan arranged on three floors, including a

basement. The gallery's Gothic echoes allow it to establish a dialogue with other important Ottawa buildings, including the Notre-Dame Cathedral Basilica and the Library of Parliament, and are particularly evident in the modern-style pinnacles that culminate in a monumental spire. However, the building also resembles a cathedral in its actual layout, which features a sort of long "nave" with huge windows.

The extensive use of glass allows visitors to maintain unbroken contact between the inside and outside of the building.

246-247 and 247 The National Gallery of Canada presents an extensive overview of art of various periods and geographic origins. Much of the collection is dedicated to Canadian art, especially of the 19th century, but it also features many 20th-century works, including a huge wall drawing, on the ground floor, by the conceptual artist Sol LeWitt, displayed next to a statue by the American minimalist sculptor Carl André.

National Gallery of Canada

In addition to the galleries, which cover an area of over 130,000 sq. ft (12,077 sq. m), the complex also has a series of large, well-lit covered courtyards. The largest of these is the Great Hall, at the end of long and very spectacular corridor, which allows access to the display floors. The first floor is home to the Canadian Galleries, displaying works by Canadian artists, and part of the collection of international contemporary art. The second floor is also dedicated to contemporary art, with areas specifically designed for video art, and large thematic sections on ancient and modern European art.

The most striking feature of the National Gallery of Canada is its structure, for the entire building is

constituted by steel frames punctuated by imposing columns, creating a dual sensation of monumentality and lightness. The spires formed by the glass and steel framework create a sort of "cut-glass pyramid," giving rise to a modern Gothic style. However, the stained-glass windows of the past are replaced by transparent glazing, allowing visitors to enjoy scenic views.

The display areas also house a rich collection of drawings and engravings covering a period stretching from ancient times to the present day.

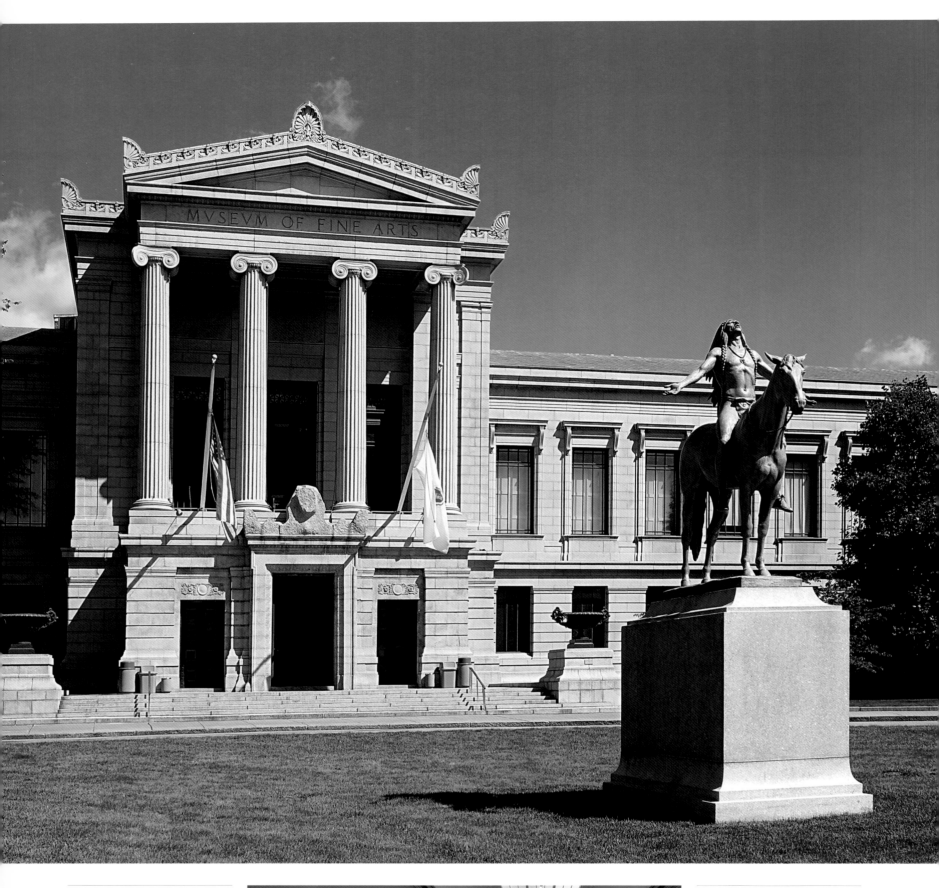

248-249 Despite its considerable length (around 500 feet), the façade of the Boston Museum of Fine Arts comprises an entrance portico flanked by two avant-corps, which lighten the overall effect. The Neoclassical-style building was built between 1907 and 1909 under the direction of architect Guy Lowell. The Appeal to the Great Spirit bronze equestrian statue stands in front of the museum. Dedicated to the Native American people, the work was cast by Cyrus Dallin in 1909.

248 bottom and 249 bottom The famous collection of ancient Egyptian art of the Museum of Fine Art is one of the highlights of this prestigious Boston institution and is housed on the second floor of the building.

249 top This drawing by I.M. Pei shows the extension of the building, achieved by the addition of the spacious and well-lit West Wing, which is used to stage special exhibitions. The wing is visible on the left of the main body of the building.

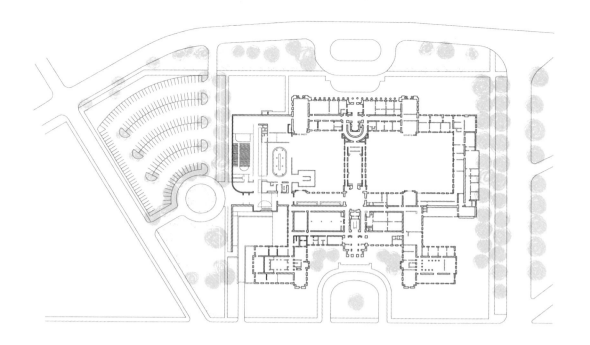

Museum of Fine Arts

BOSTON, UNITED STATES

The Boston Museum of Fine Arts ranks high among the United Sates' great museums because of its comprehensive and irreplaceable collections. These include many renowned masterpieces of art, archaeology and design, ranging from prehistoric art to contemporary artistic production from all over the world. The museum was founded in February 1870 and its first home opened to the public in 1876. These premises were in Copley Square and were a red brick Gothic Revival building with terracotta decorations designed by the architects John H. Sturgis and Charles Brigham. The first phase of construction was completed between 1876 and 1890, and work was recommenced several times in the attempt to keep up with the constant and extraordinary growth of the collection. However, at the end of the 19th century it was decided to move the museum to a new site, as it was impossible to extend the Copley Square premises any further.

In keeping with this decision to move, the collections were transferred between 1907 and 1909 to their current home in the imposing and magnificent Neo-Classical building on Huntingdon Avenue. The new museum was designed by the architect Guy Lowell in a style that reflected the fashion of the time: the façade of the marble and granite building has imposing columns surmounted by a pediment, which stands in front of a central dome, while the galleries are arranged around two inner courtyards. The museum's former premises were subsequently transformed into the Copley Plaza Hotel.

The new quarters were not to remain adequate in size for very long. The museum's collections continued to grow and so also did the building, with expansions almost always financed by large donations by private benefactors. In 1915 the Robert Dawson Evans Wing was opened and in 1921 the American artist John Singer Sargent frescoed the walls of the rotunda

and colonnade. Lowell also built the Decorative Arts Wing, which was opened to the public in 1928 and which was extended by the Forsyth Wickes Addition during the 1960s. The School of the Museum of Fine Arts, where many important American contemporary artists trained, was also moved to Huntington Avenue and was renovated during the 1980s.

However, the museum's most important and best known expansion, which allowed it to increase its exhibition space significantly, was that designed by the Chinese-born architect I.M. Pei, widely known for his pyramidal entrance to the Louvre and his redesign of the underground entry areas.

Museum of Fine Arts

250 and 251 Two of the finest architectural and artistic features of the Museum of Fine Arts are the Rotunda and the monumental staircase that leads to it, which are not only extremely refined and well-balanced, but also exquisitely decorated. One of the medallions of the decorative scheme depicts a highly significant theme for this important museum: Athena protecting Architecture, Painting and Sculpture from the ravages of time. The painted decorations are the work of John Singer Sargent, who worked on them between 1916 and 1925 and executed the frescoes in the main rooms of the museum. Guy Lowell, the museum's architect, also designed many other important buildings in New England.

252-253 and 253 top
The extremely linear style of I.M. Pei's architecture is clearly evident in every single detail of the museum's West Wing. This photograph shows the entrance lobby with the escalator leading to the gallery above. This large gallery, visible on the top right, is ideal for housing works of art, due to its excellent natural lighting and rational design.

253 bottom The Bauhaus influence is easily recognizable in the exterior of the West Wing: I.M. Pei's extreme rationalism makes few concessions to "non-functional" features.

Museum of Fine Arts

The Boston Museum's new West Wing, opened in 1981, was conceived as a small new museum, independent but connected to the White Wing of the historic main building, with which it blends, preserving its symmetry and structure and even presenting the same gray granite exterior. The museum's collections are extremely rich and varied. The American art section is particularly representative and comprises works ranging from ancient pottery to paintings by artists such as John Singer Sargent, John Singleton Copley,

more recent period extending from the Renaissance to the 20th century, and features masterpieces ranging from paintings by Rogier van der Weyden and Rosso Fiorentino to extraordinary works by Picasso and Matisse, as well as drawings and engravings by Dürer, Goya, Munch and Degas, to name but a few. The collection of approximately 1600 paintings includes many 19th-century French works that allow visitors to admire the pictorial conquests and revolutions of the Barbizon, Impressionist and post-Impressionist artists, with

Georgia O'Keeffe, Arthur Garfield Dove, Charles Sheeler and Stuart Davis.

The ancient art section is home to an impressive array of important exhibits from all over the world: Egypt, Greece, Etruria and Rome, but also Asia, Africa and Oceania. Indeed, the museum's collection of Asian art, and Japanese art in particular, is considered the most outstanding in the United States. The section dedicated to European art documents a

numerous paintings by Jean-François Millet and Claude Monet. The contemporary art section, covering the period from the 1960s to the present, features works by Andy Warhol, Jim Dine, Georg Baselitz, Mona Hatoum, David Hockney, Anselm Kiefer and Christian Boltanski. The museum also has significant collections of textile and fashion arts and musical instruments, containing rare pieces from all over the world, dating from ancient to modern times.

Metropolitan Museum of Art
NEW YORK, UNITED STATES

The Metropolitan Museum of Art in New York is one of the most important museums in the United States and the largest art museum in the whole of North America. It owes its foundation to a group of American art lovers, who decided to establish an institution to bring art and art education to their fellow citizens. The Met was founded in 1870 and during the same year the museum was officially recognized by the State of New York and assumed the name by which it is still known today. Its first temporary premises were in Fifth Avenue, but they soon proved to be too small and larger ones were sought. In 1880 the collections were transferred to their permanent home in Central Park: a then red-brick Gothic Revival building with slate roof and skylights, designed by the architects Calvert Vaux and Jacob Wrey Mould. The façade was designed in 1895 by Richard Morris Hunt, although it was not completed until the beginning of the 20th century, along with other imposing work to extend the museum.

In 1913 north and south wings were added, to the design of architects McKim, Mead and White, but the periodic succession of extensions (which will undoubtedly continue) means that hardly anything of the original building can be seen from the outside today. The sole surviving traces can be found in the Robert Lehman Wing – a distinctive pyramidal structure designed by Kevin Roche John Dinkeloo and Associates and opened to the public in 1975 – where its west façade is still visible, and in the Carroll and Milton Petrie European Sculpture Court in the southern wing of the building. Several other extensions have been added recently to house the various collections, making extensive use of glass and skylights. Indeed, the complex has been extended to the northeast (1979), northwest (1980), south (1982) and southwest (1987), enclosing an area of 2 million sq. ft (185,000 sq. m) and extending 1320 ft (400 m) from end to end. It is as though 19 identical buildings had been added to Vaux and Wrey Mould's original one!

The growing prestige of the new museum led many collectors to donate their collections to it.

254 and 254-255 The Metropolitan Museum of Art, is located on the edge of Central Park, in the heart of Manhattan, and is one of the largest and most important American museums. It is still housed in the original large Gothic Revival building, designed by Calvert Vaux and Jacob Wrey Mould, which has nonetheless been extended greatly on all sides, except the main façade.

255 bottom The constant growth of its collections obviously means that the Metropolitan Museum of Art is subject to periodic structural expansions. For this reason the building has many facets visible from different viewpoints, as shown by these two glimpses of the modern Roof Garden (left) and the Neoclassical façade (right).

256-257 The Engelhard Court, in the American Wing, is a very evocative spot. The northern wall of the huge space, arranged like a garden and furnished with wooden benches, is formed by the façade of the Wall St. branch iof the United States Bank, which was salvaged and reconstructed in the museum.

Metropolitan Museum of Art

256 bottom The Metropolitan Museum's collection, which initially consisted of just 174 paintings, now comprises over 2 million works of art from all periods, stretching from ancient to modern times. The museum has over 20 thematic sections, including the prestigious one dedicated to European art, and particularly ancient sculpture,

which is housed in the recently redesigned New Greek and Roman Galleries.

257 A huge atrium forms the entrance hall of one of the most important museums in the world: the Metropolitan Museum of Art in New York, which was founded in 1870 by a group of American art lovers.

They included Catharine Lorillard Wolfe, who bequeathed 143 masterpieces of the Barbizon school, and Erwin Davis, who donated two great works by Manet. The original nucleus of the museum's art collections consisted largely of two collections of Dutch, Flemish and Italian paintings. In 1874 the museum received a donation of a large collection of Greek and Cypriot antiquities, and in 1901 Jacob Roger, a famous locomotive manufacturer, gave it a generous endowment that allowed it to become autonomous.

The early years of the 20th century also marked the start of a succession of various strategies and cultural policies applied by the museum's various directors and aimed at expanding its collections, which were backed by the city government and the country's leading politicians. A key figure in this process was the museum's president John Pierpont Morgan, a great magnate who appointed important businessmen and collectors to the board of trustees with the aim of obtaining the world's greatest works of art for the museum. In this he was also assisted by the famous art critic Roger Fry, who enterprisingly managed to channel works by Giotto, Carpaccio, Bosch, Bruegel, Delacroix, Tintoretto and Rubens into the collection, and subsequently by Bryson Burroughs, the curator of the museum's painting section. The uninterrupted series of important donations included the large collection of Benjamin Altman – the owner of a chain of department stores – composed of Chinese porcelain, Renaissance sculpture, jewelry and numerous paintings; that of Louise Havemeyer and Henry Osborne, consisting of around 150 works of 19th-century French art; and that of J. Pierpont Morgan Jr., comprising about 7000 pieces of Byzantine art.

258-259 and 259 top The Carroll
and Milton Petrie European
Sculpture Court was designed as
a classical French garden. It
houses statues dating from the
15th to the 19th centuries, which
were originally conceived for an
outdoor setting.

Metropolitan Museum of Art

Famous donations of contemporary art include those by Gertrude Stein, who left the museum the portrait that Picasso painted of her in 1906, and the more recent bequest of the Jacques and Natasha Gelman Collection, which has made the museum a leading name also in the field of modern and contemporary art. These and many other bequests have allowed the Metropolitan Museum of Art to grow until reaching its current dimensions, comprising not only a rich section dedicated to European painting, but also superb collections of Greek and Roman, pre-Columbian, ancient Near Eastern,

258 bottom After crossing the great entrance hall, the interior of the building maintains the promises of its Neoclassical façade: in this view a dignified series of columns blends perfectly with the collection of Greek and Roman art housed on the second floor.

Islamic, Egyptian, Chinese and Japanese art. There are also important sections featuring arms and armor, decorative arts from the Middle Ages to modern times, musical instruments and costume history, as well as the very substantial and far-ranging sections dedicated to American art up until the present day. The Metropolitan Museum is an extremely rich and comprehensive museum complex, which also stages around 300 temporary exhibitions each year, bearing witness to its dynamic cultural activities.

259 bottom The large hall housing the reconstructed Temple of Dendur, from Nubia, is decorated with pools of water, papyrus plants and imposing sculptures to create an Egyptian atmosphere. The temple was presented to the United States by Egypt in 1965 and was reassembled in the Sackler Wing of the Metropolitan Museum of Art in 1978.

Museum of Modern Art

NEW YORK, UNITED STATES

I n 1929, the year of its foundation, the Museum of Modern Art consisted of six rooms rented for galleries and offices in the Heckscher Building on the corner of 5th Avenue and 57th Street. Today it is the most important museum of modern art in the world, in terms of both the value of its collections, comprising over 150,000 works spanning a period stretching from the late 19th century to the present, and its history as a pioneering museum and leading name in 20th-century museology. MoMA's first collection was formed by merging the private collections of three great patrons of modern art – Lillie P. Bliss, Mary Quinn and Abby Aldrich Rockefeller – with the works acquired in Europe by the museum's first director, Alfred H. Barr, and was transferred to the townhouse owned by John D. Rockefeller, Jr. on West 53rd Street in 1932.

In 1939, MoMA moved again, this time to a six-story building designed by the architects Philip Godwin and Edward Durrell Stone, with the famous garden by John McAndrew. The same year was marked by an exceptionally important acquisition, which is perhaps the most emblematic of the entire collection: Picasso's *Les Demoiselles d'Avignon*, a key painting for the understanding and the development of all modern art. The collections expanded at an increasingly rapid pace, accompanied by the establishment of the Mies van der Rohe Archive, the Department of Drawing and the museum's library. Consequently, more space was required and the architect Cesar Pelli was commissioned to extend the west wing of the museum in 1984. However, by the 1990s the problem was back and in 1997 a competition was announced for the design of a new museum building, which necessarily entailed the temporary abandon of the historic premises.

The winner was the Japanese architect Yoshio Taniguchi and the completely renovated museum reopened in 2004 on the 75th anniversary of its foundation, following four years of work (during which the collections were transferred to their temporary home in MoMA QNS in Long Island City, Queens). The building, dedicated to David and Peggy Rockefeller, boasts six stories of display space, covering a total area of around 630,000 sq. ft (58,250 sq. m), in which huge loft-style rooms suitable for large installations alternate with smaller and more intimate rooms and galleries.

260 MoMA, which reopened in 2004 in its new Manhattan premises designed by Yoshio Taniguchi, covers an area of around 700,000 sq. ft (65,000 sq. m), *distributed over 5 floors housing galleries, offices, educational areas, an auditorium, a library, an archive and the Abby Aldrich Rockefeller Sculpture Garden.* *261 Taniguchi's design for MoMA features entrances on 53rd and 54th Streets. The glass and steel structural elements are visible from the outside.*

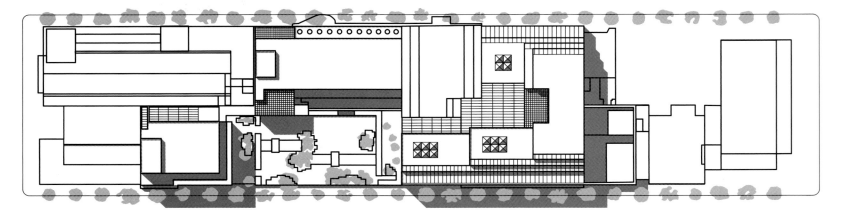

Museum of Modern Art

262 top and 262-263 The center of the huge entrance hall is dominated by Broken Obelisk (1967) by American artist Barnett Newman (1907–70), who was a major exponent of abstract expressionism and color field painting, along with Mark Rothko, Ad Reinhardt and Clyfford Still. The large sculptures and installations typical of modern and contemporary visual art are housed in the double-height loft-like space on the second floor of the museum.

262 bottom Taniguchi's winning design for the new museum premises, which won against entries by prestigious architects such as Bernard Tschumi and Rem Koolhaas was chosen for its simplicity and minimalist lightness. Following his victory, the architect eloquently explained, "If you give me enough money, I'll design you a beautiful building. If you give me more, I'll make it disappear."

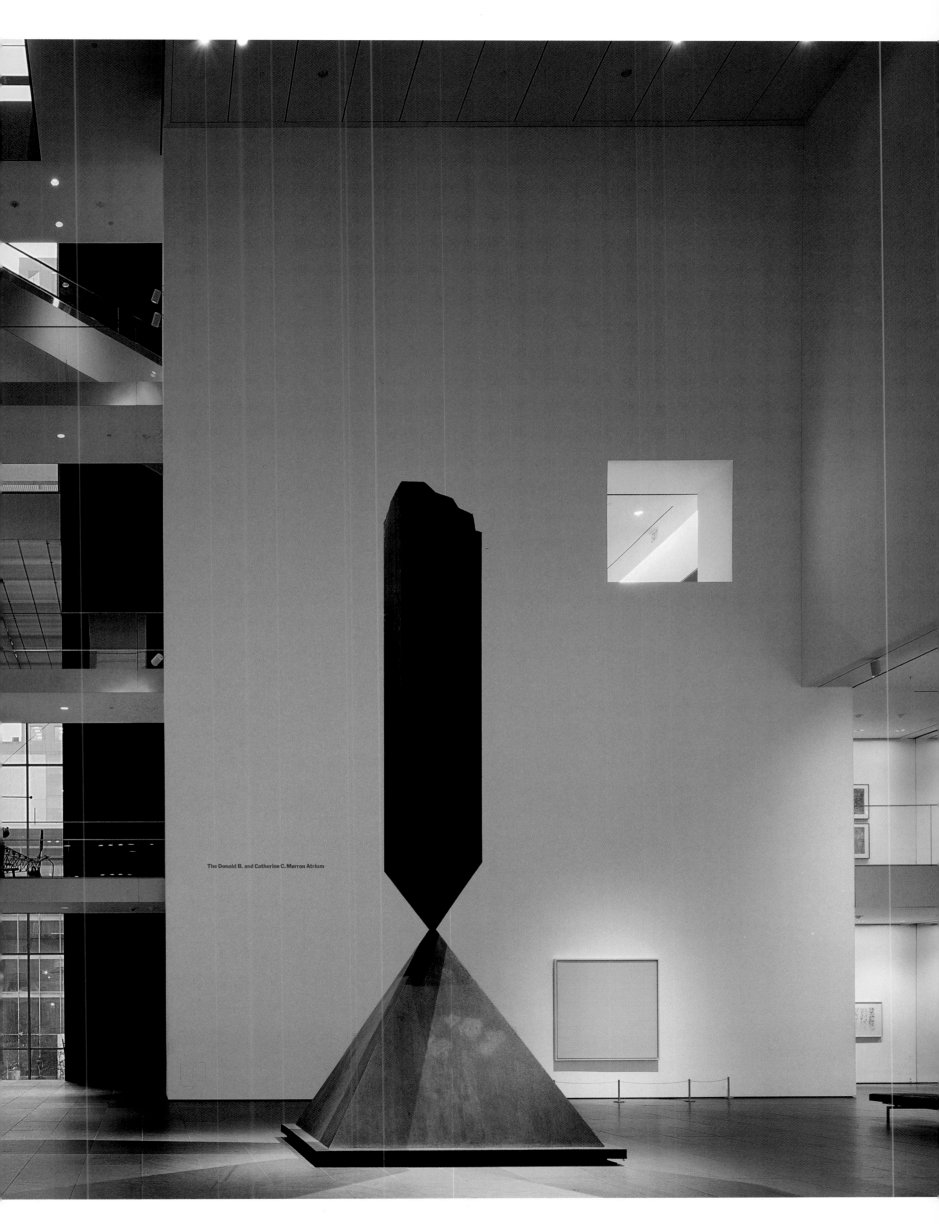

The Donald B. and Catherine C. Marron Atrium

Museum of Modern Art

264 The Sculpture Garden was opened in 1939 and, in 1953, was named after Abby Aldrich Rockefeller, the great American collector and one of the museum's founders. The garden still preserves its original design by Philip Johnson and offers glimpses of the exhibition halls through the large windows.

265 top and bottom Despite its apparently linear design, the David and Peggy Rockefeller Gallery Building is actually a fairly complex structure.

The main collection is housed on six display floors, while the top story – large enough to house three separate exhibitions – is used for temporary shows and is illuminated by the natural light that streams through skylights.

266 The spacious rooms housing the design section, which includes a collection of chairs by Rietveld, Guimard and Henry van der Velde, have been enriched with recent acquisitions allowing visitors to trace the main developments in the field of decorative arts during the 20th century.

266-267 and 267 bottom right One of the museum's most important department is that of Architecture and Design, established in 1932, which offers an overview of the developments in the sector from Art Nouveau, through Bauhaus and Rationalism, right up to the latest trends.

267 bottom left One of MoMA's most important works is the sculpture Unique Forms of Continuity in Space (1913) by Umberto Boccioni, one of the leading exponents of the Italian Futurist movement. The sculpture represents a marching figure, forged by wind and speed.

All of the areas, specifically devised and designed to house the museum's collections, are pervaded by a uniform geometric linearity, without any curved lines or spectacular architectural devices.

Taniguchi designed the Donald B. and Catherine C. Marron Atrium as a true urban space, as though it were a continuation of the street. The focus of the structure is a platform suspended 110 ft (33.5 m) above street level, which provides access to the three possible itineraries of the contemporary art sections. The large glazed areas offer fantastic views of the Sculpture Garden from both the atrium and the stairs.

Opposite the Rockefeller Building is the new Lewis B. and Dorothy Cullman Education and Research Building, housing the areas dedicated to educational and research activities, including an a huge auditorium, an expanded library and archives, and a reading room. Taniguchi has maintained Johnson's original 1953 design of the Abby Aldrich Rockefeller Sculpture Garden, while extending it and adding a terrace, which is now part of the museum's restaurant. As the posters of the museum's reopening media campaign plastered all over the city announced, "New York is Modern Again," and MoMA has retained this allure due to the presence of masterpieces such as *The Starry Night* by Van Gogh, *The Dream* by Henri Rousseau, *The Red Studio* by Matisse, *Les Demoiselles d'Avignon* and *Night Fishing* by Pablo Picasso, and *The City Rises* by Umberto Boccioni, along with other important works by Kazimir Malevich, Jackson Pollock and Jasper Johns.

Museum of Modern Art

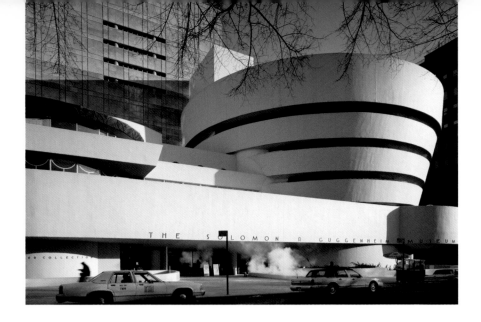

Solomon R. Guggenheim Museum

NEW YORK, UNITED STATES

In the world of modern and contemporary art, the Solomon R. Guggenheim Museum, located on New York City's upper Fifth Avenue, overlooking Central Park, remains iconic both for its structure and its collections.

Solomon R. Guggenheim (1861-1949), the museum's founder, was a rich industrialist and philanthropist who started to become interested in modern art during the late 1920s. Guided by the shrewd advice of a young German artist called Hilla Rebay, Guggenheim commenced purchasing works by living artists who were already important avant-garde figures, but had not yet achieved critical and public acclaim. In 1930 his collection was installed in an apartment at the Plaza Hotel, at Fifth Avenue and Central Park South, and Hilla Rebay started to organize small exhibitions for the public, including a loan exhibition entitled "The Solomon R. Guggenheim Collection of Non-Objective Paintings" that traveled to various American cities.

Over the following years new acquisitions and the growing importance of the collection led to the need to find a suitable location for its permanent housing and display. In 1937 the Solomon R. Guggenheim Foundation was established with the aim of the "promotion and encouragement and education in art and the enlightenment of the public." The intention to establish a museum became increasingly realistic following an agreement with New York City Council. In June 1943, Solomon Guggenheim and Hilla Rebay (who had been appointed curator of the Foundation) wrote to Frank Lloyd Wright, the foremost contemporary American architect, asking him to design the museum. Following several controversies, a suitable site was found for the building, although construction did not commence until 1957, partly owing to conflict between the intentions of Wright and the wishes of his patrons. The museum was completed in 1959, ten years after the Guggenheim's death, to whom it was dedicated as a tribute and a memorial. Wright never had the chance to see his work finished either; he died a few months before the inauguration.

The museum opened to the public on October 21, 1959, accompanied by much consternation but also great enthusiasm, for its structure was entirely unprecedented and the innovativeness and originality of the architecture were even more striking in comparison to the regular geometric forms of the surrounding buildings. In designing the museum, Wright tried to avoid creating a building with a static geometric form, striving instead to create a structure able to express the formal sculptural quality typical of living and organic elements both outside and inside. The form that provided his inspiration for the design was a snakelike, curving "reversed spiral" built in white concrete, whose diameter increases as it rises and whose coils create the four display levels. In addition to its external impact, the most innovative feature – which still strikes visitors to the museum – is the spiral ramp that acts as a gallery for the works. Inside the building the spiral opens onto a large central space, which is topped by a glass dome about 100 ft (30.5 m) above the ground.

268 The museum's sculptural, circular structure creates a strong contrast with the regular forms of the neighboring buildings.

269 The unusual impact of the exterior of the building is principally due to Frank Lloyd Wright's intriguing horizontal alternation of solids and voids derived from the reversed spiral form that inspired his design.

270-271 The center of the atrium offers fine views over the display floors and the alternating series formed by the six sloping levels.

272 *The interior of the Solomon R. Guggenheim Museum in New York engages the visitor in a totally untraditional way, for the works on display become part of* an installation, or a wider work of art, in which the descent through the various levels implies not only the perception of the exhibits, but also of the architectural space.

273 top *One interesting aspect of Wright's design is the fact that the works displayed on the other floors can be seen from any point in the gallery.*

273 bottom *The museum entrance consists of a large foyer – depicted here from above – where several works are displayed.*

Solomon R. Guggenheim Museum

Visitors descend the slightly sloping ramp, walking through the display area consisting of over 70 niches and small galleries, thus establishing a more absorbing relationship with the works.

In 1993 the museum gained urgently needed additional exhibition space with construction of the adjoining Tower Galleries, designed by the architect Charles Gwathmey. This ten-story building is located behind Wright's original structure.

Hilla Rebay was succeeded by other important directors, including Thomas M. Messer and Thomas Krens, who not only added to the Foundation's collections, but also laid the foundations of the current international network of Guggenheim museums of modern and contemporary art, located in Bilbao, Berlin, Las Vegas and also Venice. Indeed, Peggy Guggenheim, Solomon's niece, bequeathed her far-

ranging collection to the Foundation, on the condition that it remained in her museum-home in Venice.

The Guggenheim is home to many masterpieces, ranging from historical avant-garde works of the early 20th century to 21st-century pieces; they include a rich collection of works by important artists such as Paul Klee, Pablo Picasso, Georges Braque, Piet Mondrian, Joan Miró and Marc Chagall. The museum devotes a special section to the Panza di Biumo Collection of Minimalist and Conceptual Art, while another section houses the Justin K. Tannhauser Collection, donated to the museum in 1976 and comprising works by Impressionist and post-Impressionist artists such as Paul Cézanne, Edgar Degas, Paul Gauguin, Édouard Manet, Pierre-Auguste Renoir and Henri de Toulouse-Lautrec.

Smithsonian Institution

WASHINGTON D.C., UNITED STATES

The Smithsonian Institution has a unique history among museums. In 1846, James Smithson stipulated in his last will and testament that if his nephew should die without heirs, his entire estate should go to the United States, specifying that it should be used to found an educational establishment for the "increase and diffusion of knowledge." Smithson, a natural son of the Duke of Northumberland, was raised in France, became a scientist and, curiously, never visited the United States. The institution his legacy made possible retains its original headquarters on the National Mall in Washington, D.C. The Smithsonian Castle, designed by James Renwick in Norman style (a combination of Late Romanesque and Early Gothic), was completed in 1855. The Castle's silhouette has become the symbol of Smithsonian Institution, today one of the world's largest museum networks, comprising 19 different museums, home to over 142 million objects. In addition to the galleries and numerous exhibition premises,

the Institution houses a series of 9 prestigious research centers that are also engaged in training and educational activities aimed at fueling the love and study of the arts, science and American history. It also operates the National Zoological Garden.

Nine of the Smithsonian Institution's museums are situated on the Mall, between the Washington Monument and the Capitol, while a three-level underground complex houses two more museums and the S. Dillon Ripley Center, comprising the International Gallery, offices and classrooms. Five of the remaining museums and the zoo are situated in other areas of Washington, D.C., and the Institution even has two museums in New York City: the Cooper-Hewitt National Design Museum and the National Museum of the American Indian. Most of the Institution's museums are dedicated to American history, society and culture: two of the most representative are the National Museum of American History and the Smithsonian American Art Museum.

274 top The site of the
Smithsonian Institution, to the west
of the Capitol, could not be more
monumental. However, it is
actually home to only half of the
Institution's museums.

274 bottom The Art and Industries
Building forms part of the original
museum nucleus of the Smithsonian
Institution. It was built in 1880 and
is considered the masterpiece of
architect Adolf Cluss.

274-275 This view from the south
side of the National Mall
encompasses the most important
part of the complex, with the Art
and Industries Building (center);
the Smithsonian Castle, completed

by James Renwick in 1855 (upper
left); and the small but elegant
entrance pavilion of the multi-
domed National Museum of
African Art, which became part of
the Smithsonian Institution in 1979.

The National Museum of American History opened to the public in January 1964, as the National Museum of History and Technology, and assumed its current name in 1980. President Dwight D. Eisenhower authorized the foundation of the museum, allocating a large sum for its construction, which commenced in 1958. The architectural firm of McKim, Mead and White developed the original design, and the museum's somewhat modified appearance is due to a recent renovation and rebuilding project. In 1980, the museum was renamed the National Museum of American History, to reflect more closely the sense and purpose of its collections, which are entirely dedicated to recounting, collecting and conserving all kinds of objects important for understanding the history of the American people.

The Smithsonian American Art Museum is, as its name suggests, dedicated specifically to American art. The origins of the museum's collection date back to 1829, making it America's first federal art collection, and it became one of the central components of the Smithsonian Institution in 1849, the year of its foundation. The collection began modestly when a Washingtonian named John Varden set out to form a permanent museum for the nation with his art collection. The museum's first premises were Varden's own home, but in 1841 the collection was transferred to the Patent Office Building,

276 The Donald W. Reynolds Center is one of the finest buildings of the Smithsonian Institution. It is now home to the American Art Museum and was one of Washington's first public buildings, completed in 1867. The portico of its main façade was inspired by the Parthenon in Athens and gives the building a very austere appearance that is well suited to the importance of its collections. Indeed, the museum possesses 39,000 works of art, including the most famous portrait of George Washington.

277 A handsome octagonal skylight lights the Great Hall of the Reynolds Center, which is also home to the National Portrait Gallery, while the elegant stuccowork adorning the ceiling conceals a brick vault. Due to its particular architectural value, the building (designed by Robert Mills, now considered one of America's architectural geniuses) was included in an extensive scheme to revitalize downtown Washington D.C. that was implemented during the 1990s.

Smithsonian Institution

where it is housed today. However, it was subsequently moved to the Smithsonian Castle and, following a fire, many of the works were loaned to other institutions before their final return to their current home.

Another important part of the Smithsonian Institution is the extremely popular National Air and Space Museum – dedicated to the history of flight, aviation and space travel – which is one of the most visited museums in the world. One of its highlights is the original Ryan NYP aircraft known as *The Spirit of St. Louis* which in May 1927, together with its famous pilot Charles Lindbergh, made history for completing the first non-stop flight from Paris to New York. This

adventure alone testifies to how the conquest of the skies totally changed humankind's way of life, commencing with the conception of distance. However, the museum also recounts the true roots of the history of flight in the form of the most famous airplane of all times: the original *Wright Flyer*, designed and built by the Wright brothers. On December 17, 1903, this airplane made the first sustained (though very brief) and controlled flight in history. The museum has over 20 large halls that trace the history of flight from these early adventures to the military aeronautical feats of the 1930s, fighter planes, and freight aircraft. Of course, there is also a section dedicated to space exploration.

278 top and 278-279
The National Air and Space
Museum is a veritable temple of
the history of aviation, with 22
exhibition rooms arranged on 2
floors. The building, situated at
the southern end of the National
Mall, celebrated its 30th
anniversary in 2006. Indeed, it was
inaugurated in 1976, 30 years
after the birth of the original core
of its extensive collection.

278 center One of the most
interesting buildings of the
entire complex stands just west
of the Air and Space Museum:
the Hirshhorn Museum,
expressly designed by Gordon
Bunshaft to house an important
collection of modern art. This
explains its futuristic
appearance of a huge open
cylinder raised on four massive
"legs."

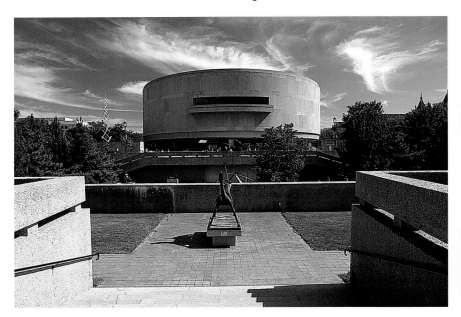

Another interesting museum of the Smithsonian
complex is the more recent Hirshhorn Museum and Sculpture
Garden, opened to the public in 1974. The museum was
made possible by the generosity and passion for art of
Joseph H. Hirshhorn, who gave his entire collection to the
Smithsonian in 1966.

The museum building, designed by Gordon Bunshaft,
is almost sculptural in appearance and has an outdoor area
entirely dedicated to modern and contemporary sculpture.
The Hirshhorn Collection comprises over 11,000 works by
the most famous and representative names of American
and international modern art, including Henry Moore,
Arshile Gorky, Alexander Calder, Alberto Giacometti and
Pablo Picasso.

Smithsonian Institution

278 bottom Situated opposite the Hirshhorn Museum (the photograph was taken in front of the building, looking toward the National Archives Building, visible in the background), the Sculpture Park is home to works by artists including Alexander Calder and Auguste Rodin.

279 bottom The Air and Space Museum houses a sculpture by the great American artist Alexander Calder, whose name is also connected with the museum through one of his paintings, which was reproduced as a print in 1976 to celebrate its opening.

Rock and Roll Hall of Fame and Museum
CLEVELAND, UNITED STATES

The Rock and Roll Hall of Fame and Museum was founded in Cleveland, which is very fitting as the term "rock and roll" was coined in the city in the mid Fifties to denote a style of music that subsequently became enormously successful throughout the United States and the whole world.

In 1983 record executive Ahmet Ertegün had the idea of founding the museum. Over the following years he and a group of enthusiasts and music industry professionals established the Rock and Roll Foundation and started to collect the funds and support necessary to found the museum. In 1986 the city of Cleveland was selected from an array of possible candidates,

and the following year the famous Chinese-born American architect I.M. Pei was commissioned to design the building that would house it.

Pei, who confessed to knowing nothing about rock and roll, initially found it difficult to devise a kind of architecture able to represent such an unusual thematic museum. However, after attending a series of concerts he came to the following conclusion: "rock and roll is about energy," just like architecture. The result was this fascinating and unique museum, opened to the public in 1995, which not only houses exhibition areas, but also a study center with offices, an archive, a library and spaces for various kinds of cultural events.

280-281 Occupying a striking site on the shore of Lake Erie, the Rock and Roll Hall of Fame and Museum, with its linear, dynamic architecture, has played an important role in the revitalization of the entire Cleveland waterfront.

281 bottom The projecting surfaces and structures that the architect has used to create this temple of rock and roll form a series of geometric solids that appear to reinterpret certain themes of rationalist architecture.

282 top I.M. Pei, who confessed to knowing nothing about rock and roll, initially found the task of designing the building a difficult one. However, the result exudes dynamism and power, as he intended.

282 bottom In keeping with the spirit of the cultural institution, the atrium houses some of the stage props of U2's "Zoo TV" tour, including a "sculpture" made from old Trabant cars.

282-283 A distinctive feature of I.M. Pei's design, the pyramid recalls his new entrance for the Louvre. However, in the case of the Cleveland museum the structure is not independent, but linked to the central structure of the building.

Rock and Roll Hall of Fame and Museum

Formed by joining a series of juxtaposed geometric solids, the focus of the building is a 162-ft/50-m-high orthogonal tower that stands on the shore of Lake Erie, around which two other architectural structures, housing the display areas of the museum, are asymmetrically arranged.

In front, on the side facing the harbor, the compressed conical form of the theater is cantilevered over Lake Erie and connected to the other parts of the museum by a walkway. However, the most spectacular aspect of the building is the huge triangular-shaped pavilion that, joined to the other main structures of the museum, forms the unusual façade and main entrance of the side of the complex overlooking the public plaza, designed to stage performances, concerts and shows of all kinds.

The display areas are arranged on eight floors, of decreasing size due to their location in the tetrahedral glass

pavilion. The final room is the Hall of Fame, where visitors find themselves surrounded by fiber-optic lights. The galleries, connected by stairs and elevators, form a sort of covered square, where visitors can stop and rest. This "plaza" has a café and stores, but above all offers splendid views over the surrounding area. It is also flooded with natural light, due to a large window and the extensive use of white. The materials chosen by I.M. Pei for the construction of the museum are very simple and consist mainly of concrete clad with white-painted aluminum panels, which contrast strongly with the charcoal gray floors of the interior, and glass, which creates reflections between the inner and outer spaces of the museum. In addition to these light effects, the Rock and Roll Hall of Fame and Museum also creates sound effects, and the reverberation of the sound waves from its interior extends to the neighboring areas and the landscape, creating an even more unusual sensation.

San Francisco Museum of Modern Art
SAN FRANCISCO, UNITED STATES

The San Francisco Museum of Modern Art, also known as SFMOMA, is a museum of modern and contemporary art situated in the Yerba Buena Gardens, a recently redeveloped area whose revival was also boosted by the establishment of the new Center for the Arts. The current museum was designed by architect Mario Botta in 1995, but its origins reach back to 1935, when it first opened to the public, displaying around 40 works of art donated by Albert M. Bender. The museum subsequently started to stage a series of important exhibitions, extending its collection at the same time. It was the first museum on the West Coast to be devoted solely to 20th-century art and for the first 60 years of its life it was housed on the third and fourth floors of the War Memorial Veterans Building in Van Ness Avenue, in the heart of San Francisco.

During the 1950's the museum premises were modernized and the exhibition space was extended in order to house its constantly growing number of works. The museum was extended several more times, particularly from the 1970's, spreading from the fourth to the third floor of the building. However, at the end of the 1980's the decision was taken to abandon the Veterans Building, due to the evident need for a larger and more functional museum to display and enhance all the greatly expanded collections.

284 The San Francisco Museum of Modern Art is situated in the Yerba Buena Gardens on a corner plot between 3rd, Mina and Howard Streets. Its renovation,

completed in 1995, has led to the revival of the entire district.

285 The horizontal lines and volumes of the San Francisco

Museum of Modern Art, designed by the Swiss architect Mario Botta, contrast strongly with the surrounding urban landscape.

286 Visitors are drawn from the ground floor atrium court up to the floors of the galleries via a grand staircase. The black and white striped stone tower in Botta's signature style contrasts with the red brick façade.

287 top Natural light floods the atrium through the skylight and the stairwell. Light is a fundamental aspect of Botta's work because of its ability to link inside and outside.

287 bottom The conceptual art of Sol LeWitt, famous for his huge abstract wall drawings, creates an impressive contrast in this view of the atrium.

San Francisco Museum of Modern Art

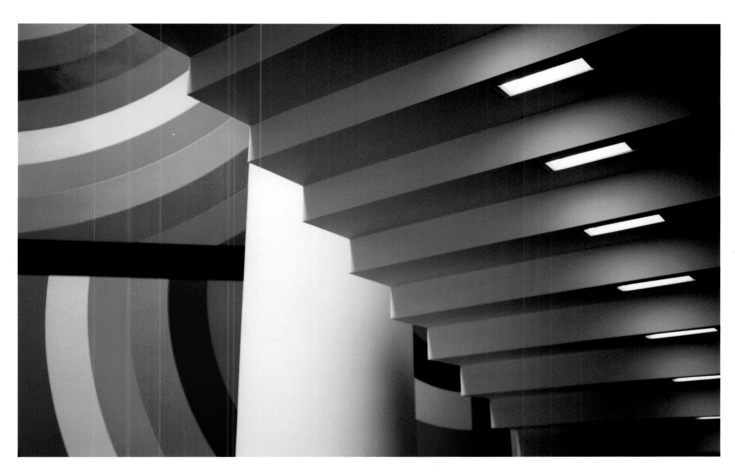

In 1988 Mario Botta was chosen to design the new museum, marking the Swiss architect's first commission in the United States. Construction commenced soon after and in 1994 the museum's works and offices were moved to the new building, which was inaugurated the following year.

Today Botta's building is one of San Francisco's most interesting and representative examples of modern architecture. It is a compact, solid structure formed by the symmetrical juxtaposition of square volumes around a central truncated cylinder.

The stepped-back brick-and-stone façade is characterized by three colors, with red bricks contrasting with the black and white bands of the cylinder, which are repeated in the pilasters, columns and walls flanking the entrance and inside the atrium. The prominent use of squares and circles and natural materials are recurrent features of Mario Botta's work that can also be seen in SFMOMA: the red bricks, like the tower, evoke medieval architecture, while the zebra stripes of the skylight tower and the columns and pilasters of the atrium are reminiscent of Siena cathedral and Moorish architecture.

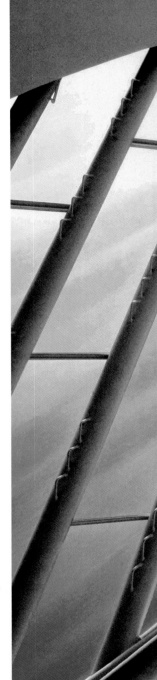

288 top The top floor is dedicated mainly to the museum's large collection of photographs and graphic art, but also houses a library with over 65,000 books, open to the public on request, and other areas for public activities.

288 bottom Two semicircular staircases ascend the skylit cylinder, giving visitors an insight into how Botta constructed the building by placing the emphasis on the central axis and center of gravity of the composition.

The brick façade conceals the concrete and steel structure of the museum, built in compliance with San Francisco's severe regulations for earthquake-resistant construction.

Another of the distinguishing features of Botta's style – derived from the architecture of Louis Kahn, for whose studio he once worked – is the role played by natural light in the spaces of the building: sunlight enters from overhead through the skylight tower, flooding the atrium and the galleries and amplified by the all-white walls. However, for Botta, light has a highly symbolic as well as a functional value. He considers museums the cathedrals of our times and, as such, believes that they must allow visitors to approach contemporary art without intimidating them, but aiding them through a quasi-spiritual contact with the buildings in which they are displayed.

In addition to the luminous spaciousness of the three display floors, which are home to around 20 galleries containing works by the greatest artists of the 20th and 21st centuries, the museum strikes visitors with the way in which its building manages to fit in and dialogue with the skyscrapers and surrounding urban fabric. While it is deliberately much lower than its towering neighbors, it nonetheless boasts a sculptural quality and a material and formal identity that allow it to stand out without being overshadowed.

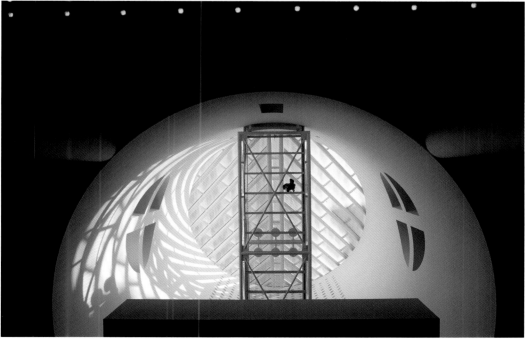

288-289 and 289 bottom Mario Botta has described the museum as a cathedral of contemporary art, in which light – as a natural element and a construction material, reflecting the influence of the architecture of Louis Kahn – becomes the symbol of the spirituality and sacredness of the building. The awe-inspiring cylindrical skylight that floods the atrium with natural light eloquently demonstrates this concept. The bridge that runs beneath it allows visitors to look down on the atrium, which is the nerve center of the building.

290-291 The museum boasts a luminous and spacious display area of 50,000 sq. ft (4650 sq. m). This space has three very large galleries of approximately 7500 sq. ft (700 sq. m) each and over 20 galleries ranging from 500 to 3500 sq. ft (46 to 325 sq. m), which are home to works by the greatest artists of the 20th and 21st centuries.

291 The first gallery floor houses selections from the permanent collection and provides space for the museum's architecture and design program; the second gallery floor displays photographs and works on paper; and the top two gallery floors accommodate temporary exhibitions and large-scale works of contemporary art from the permanent collection.

292-293 At twilight Botta's juxtaposition of symmetrical masses arranged around a cylinder is transformed as the artificial lighting is switched on, redefining the image of the entire recently redeveloped Yerba Buena area, whose revival was also boosted by the establishment of the new Center for the Arts.

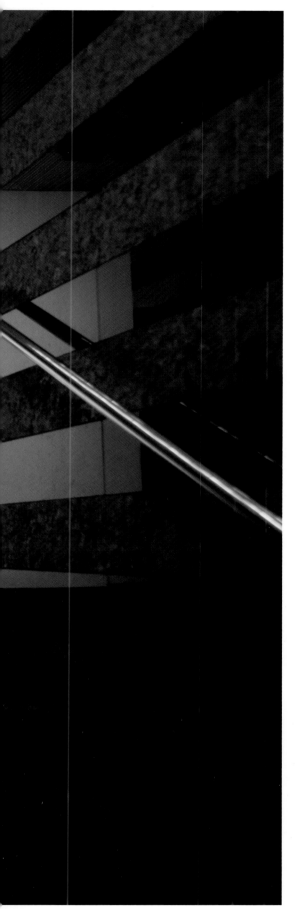

San Francisco Museum of Modern Art

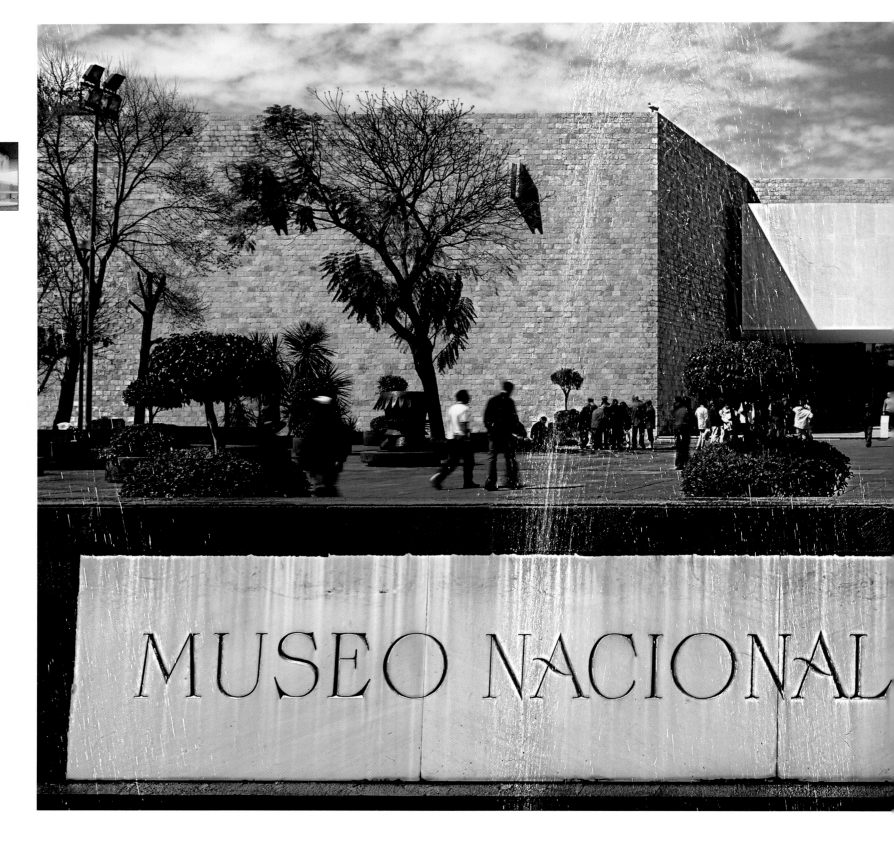

MUSEO NACIONAL

National Museum of Anthropology
MEXICO CITY, MEXICO

The National Museum of Anthropology in Mexico City was born out of the desire to recount the history and development of the Mexican civilization, from the early pre-Columbian cultures, through the display of ethnographical and anthropological exhibits. The building was constructed in 1963-64, but the origins of the collections reach back much further. Indeed, during the Spanish Conquest in the 16th century, the colonizers felt the need to study the native populations that they had recently subjugated and it was this early research that provided the anthropological basis for the

museum. One of the earliest research projects conducted with the aim of describing the history and culture of the Mexican populations was carried out by the Italian scholar Lorenzo Boturini Bernarducci, who started to gather numerous written accounts, testimonies and documents following his arrival in Mexico in 1736. However, his intentions were misconstrued and all the material was confiscated and taken to the Royal and Pontifical University, where it formed the first core of the museum's collections that subsequently began to expand at an ever-increasing rate. One of the first great boosts to the

DE ANTROPOLOGIA

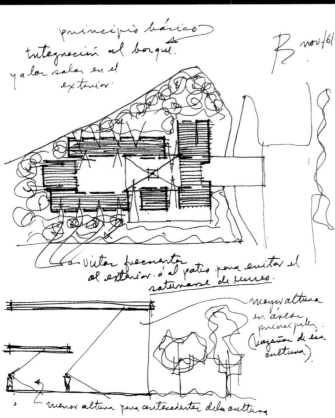

294-295 The Mexican coat of arms, which was already sacred to the Mexica tribe that subsequently became known as the Aztecs, greets visitors to the National Museum of Anthropology from the center of the building's façade. Construction of the complex commenced in 1963 on the Chapultepec hill and was completed 19 months later.

295 bottom These two sketches by architect Pedro Ramírez Vázquez show the plan and a side elevation of the future building. The project aimed to pay tribute to the native culture, which underlies the spirit of modern Mexico.

296 and 297 top From an architectural standpoint, the museum itself is a complex work of art, composed of some of the finest pieces of 1960s Mexican art, including the spectacular Paraguas ("umbrella") column

in the Gran Nayar gallery. This symbolic and monumental hammered bronze column is the work of sculptors José and Tomás Chávez Morado, and forms the focal point of the museum.

297 bottom As this drawing reveals, the original design for the Paraguas envisaged the column acting as a real umbrella, to cover visitors in the museum's courtyard. The column supports a roof measuring 275 x 170 ft (84x52 m).

National Museum of Anthropology

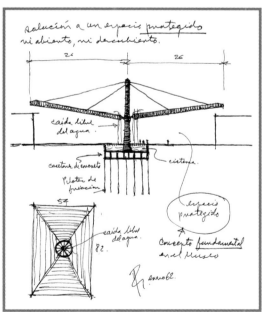

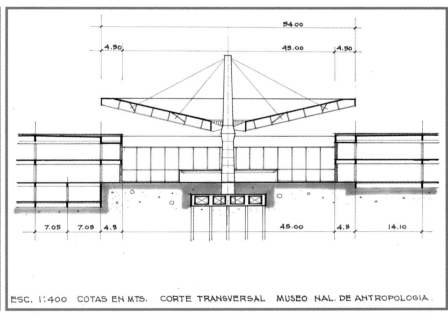

collections resulted from the order of Count Revillagigedo, the able Viceroy of New Spain, that all artifacts found during the excavations made to level the Plaza Major be delivered to the University.

However, it was the historian and politician Don Lucas Alamán who founded the Museum of Antiquities and Natural History in 1823, which officially became the National Museum in 1825 with the proclamation of the first president of Mexico, Don Guadalupe Victoria. At the time the collections consisted mainly of pre-

Columbian natural history exhibits, but the amount of material soon increased to the extent that the University was unable to display it all, and in 1865 the imported and short-lived Emperor Maximilian of Austria was forced to issue a decree designating the old building of the Casa de la Moneda – built in Baroque style in 1731 to house the mint – as the National Museum, which opened in its new premises in 1866. During the following decade the museum started to publish its annual newsletter, reflecting the constant proliferation of research and study.

National Museum of Anthropology

298 and 299 Visitors to the museum are always impressed by the exceptional exhibits (shown here, a Huastec urn or censer, bottom left; an Olmec head from Tabasco, top left; and the famous "Sun Stone," the Aztec calendar, bottom right in the background), their extremely linear architectural setting, and the layout of the display.

In 1910 problems of space and organization of the sections led to the decision to remove the natural history collections to what would officially become the National Museum of Natural History. The National Museum consequently became the National Museum of Archaeology, History and Ethnography until assuming its current name in 1939, although it did not move to its current premises until 1966. A large site overlooking Lake Chapultepec was chosen for the new building, commenced in 1963, and the architect Pedro Ramírez Vázquez was engaged to coordinate the work, which proceeded very rapidly. Indeed, just over a year and half later, the new museum was inaugurated by the Mexican president Adolfo López Mateos.

The architecture of the complex is as evocative as its contents: the careful use of planes and volumes and light and shade create arcane settings that are well-suited to the mysterious and fascinating exhibits, which include stone Olmec heads, pre-Columbian idols and enormous Mayan calendars. However, the focus of the museum is the monumental Paraguas "umbrella"-column situated in the central square of the complex. In order to provide protection from the rain for this important area of the museum (which joins the two main buildings), the architect employed the most obvious solution: an enormous umbrella. The Paraguas was initially equipped with a system to drain off the rainwater in order to avoid the accumulation of excessive loads, but was later fitted with electric pumps that constantly pour water around the central column, creating a sort of "reversed" spring. Ramírez Vázquez thus created another highly evocative space that is difficult to define, for it is neither open nor closed. The museum's unrivalled archaeological, ethnographic and artistic heritage have a display area of over 860,000 sq. ft (80,000 sq. m), of which about 475,000 sq. ft (44,125 sq. m) is roofed and 385,000 sq. ft (35,800 sq. m) is open.

BIBLIOGRAPHY

Adalgisa Lugli, Giovanni Pinna (ed.), Virgilio Vercelloni, *Tre idee di Museo*, Jaca Book, Milan 2005.

Lanfranco Binni, Giovanni Pinna, *Museo. Storia e funzioni di una macchina culturale dal Cinquecento a oggi*, Garzanti, Milan 1989.

Schubert, Karsten, *The Curator's Egg: the Evolution of the Museum Concept from the French Revolution to the Present*, One-Off Press, London 2000.

Krzysztof Pomian, *Collectors and Curiosities: Paris and Venice, 1500-1800*, (originally published in French, 1987), Polity Press, Cambridge 1990.

Basso Peressut, Luca, *Musei. Architetture 1990-2000*, Federico Motta Editore, Milan 2000.

Basso Peressut, Luca, *Il museo moderno: architettura e museografia da Auguste Perret a Louis I. Kahn*, Lybra Immagine, Milan 2005.

Olmo, Carlo (ed.), *Dizionario dell'architettura del XX secolo*, Allemandi, Turin 2000.

Gössel, Peter and Leunthäuser, Gabriele, *Architecture in the Twentieth Century*, (originally published in German, 1994), Taschen, Cologne 2001.

Michel Laclotte, *Museum Stories: Memoirs of a Curator*, (originally published in French, 2003), Abbeville Press, New York 2004.

Wilson, David M., *The British Museum: A History*, The British Museum Press, London 2002.

INDEX

PHOTO CREDITS

Tim Hiltabiddle/Agefotostock/Marka: page 272

Johanna Huber/Sime/Sie: page 178 bottom right

Hufton+Crow/View: page 145 top

Timothy Hursley: pages 218 top, 218-219, 220 bottom left and right, 221, 222, 224-225, 240-241, 241, 242 top and bottom, 243, 244 top and bottom, 245, 246-247, 247, 276 bottom left and right, 277

Javier Hinojosa: pages 294-295, 296, 297 top

Hanan Isachar/Sime/Sie: page 219 bottom right

Ian/London Aerial Photo Library/Corbis: pages 32-33

Alan Karchmer/Esto: page 158 bottom

Kunsthistorisches Museum: pages 88-89, 89

Javier Larrea/Agefotostock/Contrasto: pages 162, 163 top

Javier Larrea/Agefotostock/Marka: page 182 bottom

Courtesy of the Jewish Museum Berlin's Libeskind Building/Jens Ziehe/Jewish Museum Berlin: page 74 top

Joergensen/Laif/Contrasto: page 76 bottom left

Kaos/Sime/Sie: page 179

Brooks Kraft/Corbis: page 282 bottom

Langrock/Laif/Contrasto: pages 76 bottom right, 77

Alvaro Leiva/Agefotostock/Marka: page 191 top

Erich Lessing Archive/Contrasto: pages 11, 72-73, 98-99, 100 bottom left, 101, 189

Courtesy of the studio Daniel Libeskind: page 74 bottom right

Marcello Libra/Archivio White Star: page 90

David Mackenzie/Alamy Images: pages 152-153

Raf Makda/View: page 59 bottom

William Manning/Corbis: page 281

Daniele Mattioli/Anzenberger/Contrasto: page 151 bottom

Susy Mezzanotte: pages 157, 206 center and bottom, 212 bottom

Susy Mezzanotte/Sime/Sie: pages 208-209, 210 bottom right

Andrew Moore: page 212 center

James H Morris/Carré d'Art - Musée d'Art Contemporain de Nîmes: pages 128-129

Courtesy of the studio Moshe Safdie and Associates, Inc.: pages 219 bottom left, 223, 240

Courtesy of the Museo di Arte Moderna e Contemporanea di Trento e Rovereto: pages 166 top, 166-167, 167, 168-169, 170 top

Gerhard Murza/BPK/Archivio Scala: pages 70-71

Museum of Fine Arts, Boston: pages 248, 248-249, 249 bottom, 250 top and bottom, 253 bottom

Musée Océanographique de Monaco/Collection: page 136 bottom

Musée Océanographique de Monaco/M. Dagnino: pages 136-137, 138, 139 top, 139 bottom left and right, 140-141, 141 center bottom, 141 bottom

Netherlands Architecture Institute: pages 66 top, 66 bottom left and right

Österreichisches Staatsarchiv: page 88

Massimo Pacifico/Marka: pages 136 top, 141 top

Igor Palmin: pages 194-195, 195, 198 top, 198 bottom left and right, 199

Photolibrary: pages 150-151

Photostock: pages 190-191, 191 bottom, 192 top and bottom, 192-193

Sergio Pitamitz/Agefotostock/Marka: page 154 top

Liselotte Purper/Bpk/Archivio Scala: page 73 bottom

Courtesy of The State Pushkin Museum of Fine Arts: pages 196, 197 top and bottom

Jose Fuste Raga/Corbis: pages 158-159, 164-165

Courtesy of the Richard Rogers Partnership: pages 102 top and bottom

Christian Richters: pages 82-83, 84 bottom, 87 top left

Massimo Ripani/Sime/Sie: pages 49, 66-67, 160 bottom, 161

Hugh Rooney/Eye Ubiquitous/Corbis: page 180 left

Steve Rosenthal/www.steverosenthalphoto.com: pages 252-253, 253 top

Bill Ross/Corbis: page 282 top

Photo Rmn: pages 98-99, 99 top right, 100 bottom right, 108 bottom left and right, 110-111, 111, 112-113, 113 top and bottom, 116-117, 117 top and bottom, 118-119, 119 top and bottom

Isabel Arriero Sanchez/Cover/Contrasto: page 153 bottom

San Francisco Museum of Modern Art: page 285, 287 top

Sasse/Laif/Contrasto: page 273 bottom

Archivio Scala: pages 175 bottom, 186 center, 186-187, 260 top, 261, 262 bottom, 264, 266, 267 bottom left

Michel Setboun/Corbis: page 114

Doug Scott/Agefotostock/Contrasto: pages 202-203, 205 bottom

Giovanni Simeoni/Sime/Sie: pages 173, 204, 206-207

George Simhoni/Masterfile/Sie: pages 205 top, 210-211

Philippe Simon/Artedia: page 125 left

Massimo Siragusa/Contrasto: page 180 right

Richard Hamilton Smith/Corbis: pages 114-115

Superstock/Agefotostock/Marka: page 211 bottom

State Hermitage Museum: pages 200, 202, 210 bottom left, 212-213

M. Antoine Stinco/Les Abattoirs: pages 135 top and bottom

Michele Tabozzi: pages 15, 16, 20-21, 34-35, 35 top, center and bottom, 36 top, center and bottom, 38 top left and right, 38 bottom right, 39, 50 top, 50 bottom left and right, 51, 53 top, 53 bottom left and right, 54 top left and right, 54 bottom, 54-55, 62, 63 bottom left and right, 64, 65 top, 103, 104 top, center and bottom, 104-105, 106, 107 top and bottom, 142-143, 145 bottom, 146, 147 top, 148 right top, 148 left top, center and bottom, 149

Claude Thibault/Alamy Images: pages 108-109

Tokyo National Museum Image Archives/ www.TnmArchives.jp: pages 226, 226-227, 228 bottom left and right, 228-229, 229 top and bottom

Peter Titmuss/Alamy Images: page 211 top

The Trustees of the British Museum/The British Museum: pages 32 bottom, 33

Wes Thompson/Corbis: pages 280-281

Foto Tosi: pages 174, 175 top left and right, 178 top, 178 bottom left

Rohan Van Twest/Alamy Images: pages 258-259

Courtesy of the Unstudio: pages 82 bottom, 83 top and bottom, 84 left

Courtesy of the Unstudio/Christian Richters: pages 86, 87 top right, 87 center and bottom

V&A Images: pages 40 top and bottom, 40-41, 42, 43 top, 43 bottom right, 44 top and bottom, 44-45, 46-47, 47 top, center and bottom

Pablo Valentini/Alamy Images: page 124 bottom left

Carl Valiquet/Masterfile/Sie: page 212 top

Sandro Vannini/Corbis: page 185

Archivio Vasari: pages 184-185, 186 top and bottom

Giulio Veggi/Archivio White Star: pages 6-7, 38 bottom left, 63 top, 65 bottom

Visual&Written SL/Alamy Images: pages 8-9

Vojtech Vlk/Agefotostock/Marka: page 298

Buss Wojtek/Hoa-Qui/Hachette Photos/Contrasto: pages 200-201

Alan Wylie/Alamy Images: page 265 bottom

Yad Vashem Museum: pages 218 bottom, 220 top

Michael Yamashita: pages 254-255

Boening/Zenit/Laif/Contrasto: pages 24-25

Zentralarchiv/Bpk/Archivio Scala: page 71 bottom

Jim Zuckerman/Corbis: pages 182-183

ACKNOWLEDGMENTS

The author would like to thank:
Giovanni Pinna, Dario Pinton, Tommaso Benelli, Alessio Meoli, Alessandra Camin Galgani

The publisher would like to thank:
Ateliers Jean Nouvel, Paris, Charlotte Huisman
Mario Botta Architetto, Lugano, Elisiana Di Bernardo
Santiago Calatrava, LLC, Zürich, Angelika Kreuzer
Carré d'Art - Musée d'Art Contemporain de Nîmes, Delphine Verrières
Dale Chihuly, Seattle
Foster and Partners, London, Kathryn Tollervey
Gehry Partners, LLP, Los Angeles, Rhiannon Gharibeh
Herzog & de Meroun, Basel
INAH – Coordinación Nacional de Difusión, Mexico City, Fabiola Mosqueira
Jewish Museum, Berlin, Christiane Rütz
JPW – Johnson Pilton Walker, Sydney, Adrian Yap
Kunsthistorisches Museum mit MVK und ÖTM, Vienna, Florian Kugler
Les Abattoirs, Tolouse, Jocelyne Paris
MART, Rovereto, Attilio Begher
Moshe Safdie and Associates, Inc., Somerville, MA, Jane Baldini

Musée du Louvre, Paris, Délégation à la communication, Elisabeth Laurent de Rummel
Musée Océanographique de Monaco, Didier Théron and Michel Dagnino
Egyptian Museum, Cairo
Museum of Fine Arts, Boston, Erin M.A. Schleigh
Museum of Modern Art, New York, Carey Gibbons
Netherlands Architecture Institute, Rotterdam, Letje Lips
Österreichisches Staatsarchiv, Vienna, Leopold Auer
Pei Cobb Freed & Partners Architects LLP, New York, James Balga
Ramírez Vázquez Y Asociados, Mexico City, Pedro Ramírez Vázquez, Araceli Mendoza and Karina Garcia
Richard Rogers Partnership, London, Jenny Stephens
San Francisco Museum of Modern Art, Ann B. Gonzalez
Studio Daniel Libeskind, LLC, Berlin, Amanda Dahlquist
The State Pushkin Museum of Fine Arts, Moscow, Yuri Lukavtchenko and Inna Orn
The State Hermitage Museum, St. Petersburg, Elena Obuhovich
Tokyo National Museum and DNP Archives.com, Tokyo, Satoko Aida
UNStudio, Amsterdam, Karen Murphy
Violette Editions, London, Robert Violette
Yad Vashem Museum, Jerusalem, Susan Weisberg